The NATURAL WORLD OF
ANIMAL SEXUALITY

QUEER DUCKS

(AND OTHER ANIMALS)

ELIOT SCHREFER

ILLUSTRATIONS BY
JULES ZUCKERBERG

 Katherine Tegen Books
An Imprint of HarperCollins Publishers

Katherine Tegen Books is an imprint of HarperCollins Publishers.

Queer Ducks (and Other Animals): The Natural World of Animal Sexuality
Text copyright © 2022 by Eliot Schrefer
Illustrations copyright © 2022 by Jules Zuckerberg

Library of Congress Cataloging-in-Publication Data

Names: Schrefer, Eliot, author.
Title: Queer ducks (and other animals) : the natural world of animal sexuality /
    Eliot Schrefer.
Description: First edition. | New York : Katherine Tegen Books, [2022] | Includes
    bibliographical references and index. | Audience: Ages 14 up | Audience:
    Grades 10-12 | Summary: "A research-based exploration of queer behavior in
    different animal species is interspersed with personal anecdotes and interviews
    with scientists"— Provided by publisher.
Identifiers: LCCN 2021053153 | ISBN 9780063069503 (paperback)
Subjects: LCSH: Homosexuality in animals—Juvenile literature. | Sexual behavior
    in animals—Juvenile literature.
Classification: LCC QL761 .S36 2022 | DDC 591.56/2—dc23/eng/20211115
LC record available at https://lccn.loc.gov/2021053153

Typography by David Curtis
23 24 25 26 27 LBC 5 4 3 2 1

First paperback edition, 2023

QUEER DUCKS
(AND OTHER ANIMALS)

The NATURAL WORLD of
ANIMAL SEXUALITY

FOR
KATHI, TEDDY, AND ROY

CONTENTS

THE IMMORALITY OF PENGUINS

The Edinburgh Zoo has long been proud of its penguins. In fact, it has Europe's oldest exhibit of them, dating back to 1913. One of their current birds was even knighted! Not that he can hold a sword or anything.

How do you determine if a penguin is male or female? Turns out that it's not easy. Penguin males and females are the same size, and since their genitalia is tucked away, their sex is anyone's guess. Only a modern blood test can tell for sure. Those weren't around in 1913.

Prized animals + hard-to-determine sexes = one big old penguin sex scandal.

When the zoo received its initial population of penguins from Antarctica, they assigned them genders based on who was paired up with whom and who spent more time sitting on the eggs. The Scottish public flocked to the exhibit to meet Andrew, Bertha, Caroline, Dora, and Eric.

The trouble started soon after. First off, the zoo quickly realized that king penguins aren't fully monogamous. Following some bird canoodling, zookeepers had to regretfully inform the public that their favorite penguin couples were all cheating on one another. After seven years of observations, they also concluded they had gotten some of the sexes wrong. Actually, they got a lot of the sexes wrong. Andrew became Ann, Bertha became Bertrand, Caroline became Charles, and Eric became Erica. They had gotten it right with only one penguin, Dora.

This regendering also fixed something that had been on the zookeepers' minds—they'd been worried that some of the penguins were having homosexual sex! Phew. Not anymore, not with the new gender assignments. All fixed.

Until it wasn't. Penguins are gonna penguin, and the couples reshuffled. Everyone had had enough sex with everyone else at this point that the truth was unavoidable: the Edinburgh penguins were bisexual. The 1920s public had to come to terms with the fact that the heterosexual couple "Eric" and Dora were most definitely females, Erica and Dora. An early "lesbian" couple of penguins that had caused a stir, "Bertha" and "Caroline," were still bonded together—but actually two males, Bertrand and Charles.

This was not an isolated case. Bi penguins have been stirring things up for over a century. The very first record of same-sex sexual behavior in penguins was in 1911, when explorer George Murray Levick discovered "depraved" behavior in wild Adélies. More recently, in 2004 a pair of male chinstrap penguins at the Central Park Zoo in New York City bonded and raised a chick from an egg they'd been given to foster, inspiring the picture book *And Tango Makes Three*. Even more recently, penguin behavior sounded like it was ripped straight from a celebrity gossip site when it emerged that a "gay" couple of penguins stole an egg from a straight couple at a Dutch zoo—and then proceeded to steal an egg from a "lesbian" couple the very next year!*

It's not just penguins; a recent article in *Scientific American* notes substantiated, evidence-confirmed findings of same-sex sexual behavior in over 1,500 animal species. These aren't rare anomalies: an explosion of research over the last twenty years has shown significant amounts of same-sex sexual behavior throughout the animal kingdom. The real number of species involved is surely much higher, as studies setting out to catalog homosexual behavior in the animal world are still rare.

I really wish I'd had any inkling of all this queer behavior in nature when I was young. I was around age eleven when I started lingering over the Fruit of the Loom ads in my brother's *Rolling Stone* and realized I was attracted to other guys. An impossible thing had happened: up until then, I'd just been *me*, but now I was *gay*. To make matters worse, everything I'd ever heard indicated that gay was a horrible and unnatural thing to be. How could my internal life give me such a bummer of a plot twist? There had to be some explanation, so I looked up homosexuality in every encyclopedia I could get my hands on.

My findings were depressing. Some sources told me that homosexuality was a psychological disorder unique to humans, an illness that came to those with bad genes or who had grown up with too much attachment to their mother or father (or maybe too little, no one seemed to agree). Everywhere I looked, *unnatural* was the word that came up again and again.

The stakes of being "unnatural" were high. As I was starting college, a freshman in Wyoming, Matthew Shepard, was beaten, tortured, tied to a barbed-wire fence, and left to die because his killers hated his being gay.

---

* Note: In the rest of this book I avoid using *gay* or *lesbian* to describe same-sex sexual behavior in animals, as these terms have a whole host of connotations in humans that don't apply to the animal world. I've used the words here and elsewhere only when appropriate to convey how they were described in the press. For more discussion of sexual orientation in animals, see chapter 4.

That was only the most famous case of the hundreds of people killed each year for being queer (with Black trans women making up a disproportionate number of cases).

So what *is* natural? Many of us were brought up with the Noah's ark version of life, which tells us that the proper order of things is a bonded male-female pair for every species on earth. Darwin's theory of natural selection only seems to confirm it—by his logic, only heterosexual pairings allow for the successful propagation of genes, making them the primary driver of evolution. If natural selection is working properly, the argument goes, homosexual desire

shouldn't happen. Any sexual act that doesn't produce offspring doesn't help an animal get more of its genes into the next generation, and so is some kind of error.

These assumptions about the normalcy and biological fitness of only male-female pairings are perfectly reasonable. But what if they're also . . . wrong?

It's been an important twenty years for the field of zoology. In 1999, researcher Bruce Bagemihl released his exhaustive, meticulously researched *Biological Exuberance: Animal Homosexuality and Natural Diversity*, and over the years that followed, in species after species, across the vertebrate and even invertebrate worlds, research has shown same-sex pairings in hundreds of animal species. And not just occasional link-ups—sometimes lifelong partnerships between animals of the same sex.

The reasons for this recent bloom in reporting are twofold: research attention is finally being paid to the issue, and old taboos against publishing such results are eroding. In the past, scientists would avoid publishing on queer animal behavior because they found it shameful, or because they worried the establishment might then question the accuracy of all their results. (George Murray Levick, the explorer who wrote about homosexual behavior in Adélie penguins in 1911, hid his observations using the Greek alphabet as code—and they were still cut from the official expedition reports.) As recently as 1980, a US government document removed all references to homosexual behavior from a scientist's report on killer whales. It can't have been easy to fit a killer whale into the closet, but somehow they managed it.

There's also a problem known as confirmation bias, a psychology term that basically means we tend to find what we're looking for. Because we grew up with the assumption that those hetero Noah's ark animals are the "natural way," when we see two animals mating, most of us interpret them as a male and a female. But most animals, like the penguins, are either absolutely or nearly monomorphic: to our eyes, they don't appear different from one another.

Think of the last time you saw two animals mating, whether on the Discovery Channel or in some awkward moment while you were walking through the park. Maybe it was a couple of cats in an alley, or some pigeons on a sidewalk, or a pair of beetles—all sexually monomorphic animals, so you actually didn't know the sex of the animals you saw. Even without consciously deciding it, the story you probably told yourself in that moment was that you saw a male and a female. That could very well have been a homosexual encounter you witnessed, but because most of us are underestimating the frequency of homosexual acts in the natural world, our minds subconsciously put the sex acts we observe into the "heterosexual" column. That confirms the whole hetero system all over again and makes us even *less* likely to consider the next animal mating we witness to be same-sex.

For years, scientists' favorite explanation for same-sex penguin courting and mating was the "error hypothesis." Maybe penguins themselves couldn't recognize sex differences, they argued. (Penguins not being able to tell the difference between males and females—wow, that *would* be an evolutionary screw-up!) Or maybe it's the zoo that scrambles penguin brains and makes them do "unnatural" things. But then a definitive study of wild king penguins was launched in 2010 and found that over 28 percent of their breeding pairs were same-sex. In one stroke, that study countered both theories: these were wild penguins, so there was no supposed "zoo effect" interfering with their sexuality, and the proportion of same-sex courtships didn't match what we'd expect in the unlikely event that they truly were unable to discriminate the sex of their partners.

This is one example of a general trend in science, which is to provide negative explanations for why an animal's sexual expression or mating habits are "unnatural." There's a hormonal imbalance, the story goes, or maybe a lack of suitable sexual partners of the opposite sex, or the animal is making mistakes in choosing partners. Or queer sex is explained away as a technique to "show another animal who's boss" or as training for "proper" (i.e., straight) sex later on—disregarding that those explanations, even if true, don't make the homosexual sex any less of a sexual act. Sex between straight humans can be an act of dominance, after all, or training for future bonking . . . but it's still sex. Some of these negative explanations are true in some cases—but as we'll see, they fail to explain a wild abundance of queer animal sex and sexual identity.

Sure, you could protest that maybe the 28 percent of wild king penguins who choose partners of the same sex are just screwing up big-time, because of a bad environment, hormonal disorders, or frustration at a lack of available hetero partners. But why not consider a simpler explanation, that these male penguins desire male penguins, that these female penguins desire female penguins, just as many humans desire people of the same sex? That same 2010 study found that bonded same-sex penguin couples learn each other's calls and go to great effort to find their chosen same-sex partner in the huge crowd of over two hundred thousand birds, whatever amount of searching it takes. Just like the bonded hetero couples. All signals point to the fact that the best explanation of penguin homosexuality might also be the simplest: they desire their same-sex partner. It just makes them happy.

In this book we'll explore some negative theories about animal sexuality, but also many positive theories for why queerness is part of animals' natural state. A few examples: In the human species, homosexual males often have sisters who are more fertile than other women, and it's also been theorized that the percentage of purely same-sex-oriented individuals in an animal population is frequently similar to the mortality rate of parents; that is, that same-sex bonding builds a foster parent system into wild populations. Polyamory—the bonding of three or more animals, instead of the conventional two—can expand the effective pool of parents, increasing the survivability of offspring. There's also a theory known as "bisexual advantage," coming from data showing that fluid sexuality increases reproduction chances across a population, making bisexuality "an evolutionary optimum." (Bisexual Advantage would make a killer band name, by the way.)

It's also true, as we'll come to see, that not all animal behavior needs to have had some benefit to have evolved. Darwin's theory of evolution by natural selection got many things right, but "adaptive fitness" is not the only explanation for why an animal behaves the way it does. It's just like how some of us, say, get pleasure out of cracking our knuckles or picking our nose. No one's saying that behavior had to directly evolve; it's just the outcome of a lot of other traits (like body awareness and using up nervous energy that has no other outlet) that evolved for separate reasons. Like us, some animals simply make individual choices, and the capacity to make those choices can persist over their species' evolution, without having an evolutionary impact. This is what is called a "mentalistic" explanation for their behavior: animals might do something—like have sex with a member of the same sex—simply because they have a mind, and having that mind makes them want to. Not because they've made some grand evolutionary calculation.

These explanations don't have to cancel one another out, either! An animal's behavior can have an evolutionary explanation, a sociological explanation, *and* a mentalistic explanation. The idea that same-sex sexual behavior in animals has evolutionary explanations isn't incompatible with the idea that they also do it because they enjoy it or it makes them feel connected.

Human queerness is too complicated for us to make any sweeping conclusions about it based on animal examples. Still, there will be plenty in here that I hope helps to shed light on human sexuality. We're animals, after all, and can understand ourselves better by recognizing similarities to our animal kin.

This is partly a book for lonely eleven-year-old Eliot, who only began to see himself as worthy of full respect many years after coming out. I thought my queerness separated me from the rest of the animal world, but came to love myself once I began to feel deep in my bones that being "unnatural" didn't automatically make me bad or wrong. That's still certainly true: there's no innate link between unnatural things and wrongness. After all, reading books could be considered "unnatural," but few people argue that it's bad. Regardless, the young Eliot would have had a quicker journey to self-acceptance if he'd known the science that's in this book.

This is also a book for you, whoever you are, whether you're queer or not.* Humans as a whole need not be lonely in the natural world. Queer behavior in animals is as diverse and complex—and natural—as it is in our own species. Isn't that a relief?

---

* For an exploration of the language I'll be using to describe our states of being as they relate to sex and gender, see "What Queer Means" on page 25.

ꟾNTERLUDE

WHO I AM (AS IT PERTAINS TO THIS BOOK)

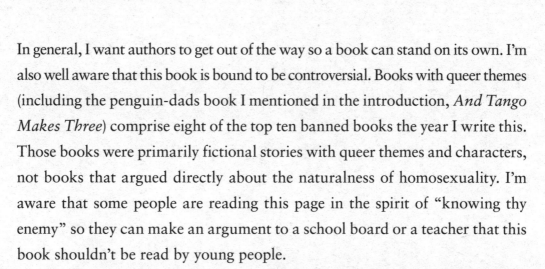

In general, I want authors to get out of the way so a book can stand on its own. I'm also well aware that this book is bound to be controversial. Books with queer themes (including the penguin-dads book I mentioned in the introduction, *And Tango Makes Three*) comprise eight of the top ten banned books the year I write this. Those books were primarily fictional stories with queer themes and characters, not books that argued directly about the naturalness of homosexuality. I'm aware that some people are reading this page in the spirit of "knowing thy enemy" so they can make an argument to a school board or a teacher that this book shouldn't be read by young people.

On the other hand, I also know that I'm just one person with one gender identity and sexual orientation, and that I'm liable to get things wrong about the experiences of others, to fail to properly consider how some of my words will land on ears that aren't like mine. So let me tell you how I identify, because knowing where I come from might help you in getting the most out of this book: I'm a white, gay, cisgender* man.

I know I'm also a little unusual in my consideration of animals. Most of my writing life has been spent writing about animals in a whole bunch of different ways, whether a fox and a rooster operating an agency to rescue animals in distress (*The Animal Rescue Agency*) or a girl relying on her bond with a bonobo ape to help both of them survive a civil war (*Endangered*). As I've visited schools for my books, I've learned that how I think about animals is outside the mainstream. I often get asked—by teachers, not kids—whether my books are arguing that animal lives are more important than human lives. I've always been a little baffled by that question. I'd never said such a thing; I'd just said that I thought animal lives were worth caring about, and that we should seriously consider modifying our behavior when that behavior does harm to them. But the question I got had an assumption beneath it, that care given to animals means less care left over for humans, and that it is therefore immoral. I emphatically disagree with that assumption. I don't think caring is a limited resource. I think the sum of care in the world can be increased. In fact, I think care for animals leads to greater care for humans, too, since we all share the natural world, and the same systems of power that endanger animals also endanger humans.

I do think animals are deserving of significant moral consideration. I hope that, a hundred years from now, we'll look back on our current practices in horror. We currently farm and kill 10,000,000,000 (yes, that's ten *billion*) land animals for food each year in the United States, in horrific conditions that it's often illegal to even film or report on because the powerful agricultural lobby doesn't want us to see what goes on inside. The number of aquatic creatures killed by industrial fishing is even higher,

---

* That means my gender identity corresponds with the sex I was assigned at birth. For more discussion of the terms I'll be using in this book, see "What Queer Means" on page 25.

estimated to be between 1,000,000,000,000 and 3,000,000,000,000 (one and three *trillion*). Trawling dredges up entire ecosystems into nets, and large ocean fish populations are at 10 percent of their pre-industrial levels. We will one day wonder how twenty-first-century humans—us—could have let that happen.

I'll also admit that I'm sloppy in that conviction, and don't always act in ways that give animals equal moral consideration. (In other words, I love cheese.) Others live their lives with more consistency in their consideration of animals, and I admire them greatly. I'm a part of the Animal Studies master's program at New York University, and have met advocates there whose passionate work on the behalf of animals inspires me. Many of them have helped me with this book.

I bring these things up as a way to let you know something that I think it's important you hear. Throughout these chapters I'll draw connections between animals and humans, between animal sexual attraction and human sexual attraction, between animal sexual identity and human sexual identity. To be compared to animals is loaded, particularly for people who have already been mockingly compared to an animal on the basis of their race, sexuality, or gender expression. I want you to know that I don't intend any negative value judgment in comparing humans to animals—in fact, I consider these links sources of comfort and wonder.

There's nothing that special about me. I'm just a doodlebug. Some people call me a maybug or a cockchafer, which is a rad name.

Okay, there is this one crazy thing that happened to me. I was hooking up with this other guy, and it was going really well, we were both really into it, but then, well . . .

My junk **BROKE** off inside his exoskeleton! Just fell right off. I guess it's still in there somewhere.

I told you!

⑀OODLEBUGS

IT TAKES A LOT OF BACKBONE TO COME OUT. OR DOES IT?

"A history of the scientific study of animal homosexuality is necessarily also a history of human attitudes toward homosexuality." —Bruce Bagemihl

August Kelch had a suspicion about what he was seeing, and he was not happy about it. The German schoolteacher and zoologist had come across what appeared to be two doodlebugs in the middle of doing the dirty. That was unseemly enough in 1834 Germany. It only got worse from there: Kelch thought it looked like two *male* doodlebugs. The insects probably would have preferred some privacy to finish up their sexy times, but Kelch seized them right up and brought the still-attached insects around to his various colleagues. We don't know what the exact words he used were, but it was probably the nineteenth-century German equivalent of "dude, are these two guys?"

(I was once in Central Park with my boyfriend, in New York City. We'd had a big picnic lunch and fallen asleep on the blanket, bellies filled with pasta salad and arms wrapped around each other. I woke up when I heard a big group of high schoolers clomp by, chattering about their upcoming Michigan soccer championships. When they neared me and my boyfriend, still entwined on our blanket, their chatter went silent. Once they were past us, I heard one of them say, in a loud whisper, "Dude, that was two *guys*." I'm very proud of that day. I'm sure we made the top five stories of their school trip.)

Those doodlebugs were indeed two guys. The scientists carefully parted the two—and the one in back's junk promptly fell off inside the one in front. Horrors. You can imagine the German scientists, wincing with their hands over their mouths. "Sorry, buddy!"

It turns out, by the way, that doodlebug sex tends to be much safer for the receiver. That makes sense when you remember that there's an exoskeleton involved. You try sticking your thing into some sharp plates of barbed chitin and see how it comes out. (Don't actually do that.)

This was a significant day for those doodlebugs, not only because one of them had his doodle snapped off. Those doodlebugs thought they were just having some hanky-panky, but it was an important day for science in general, because Kelch's realization turned into the first modern scientific account of animal homosexuality.

Kelch didn't know at the time that he was witnessing something that would go down in history. He just knew that this was nothing he thought God ought to be allowing in the natural world.

Male bugs were not meant to doodle other male bugs.

Right?

Kelch couldn't help but look closer. He noticed that the mounting bug, the one who lost his penis in the parting, belonged to a larger subspecies, the common cockchafer, and had mounted a smaller forest cockchafer. ("Cockchafer" really is another name for doodlebugs, I kid you not.) Kelch concluded that the "stronger of the two had forced itself on the smaller and weaker one, had exhausted it and only because of this dominance had conquered it, so to speak." The only way he could conceive of same-sex intercourse was as an act of rape. No male bug should give himself willingly to another male, obviously!

This question of "animal perversion" had been a hot topic among scientists for centuries, and still holds sway—consciously and subconsciously—over many of them today. There was no term "homosexual" in German or English back in 1834, when Kelch discovered the mating males. Human homosexual *acts* were recognized, however, and were considered illegal, because they fell under the umbrella of "unnatural behavior." Someone found to be consorting with a person of the same sex could be accused of indecency, or acting against God's will, or unnaturalness. These criminal categorizations for people accused of same-sex sex relied on the belief that only male-female sex was natural, and all else was perversion. This has remained a fundamental assumption of the white European world in particular. The majority of human societies throughout history were more welcoming to same-sex sexual behavior—it has been tolerated or embraced in 64 percent of them, in fact, as noted by a recent study.

We'll talk more about the history of human sexuality in chapter 4, but it's worth noting now that this hard line against queerness in dominantly Christian societies was not always the case, but the result of a rapid rise of intolerance as Europe emerged from the comparatively accepting Dark Ages. The idea that some neighbors were worthy of loving and others worthy of murder has always been part of human nature, but spread especially within the Christian worldview in the half century between 1250 and 1300, when the leaders of the nations of Europe drew power from exclusionary "us versus them" thinking. Homosexuality went from fully legal throughout Europe in 1250 to a death-penalty offense in most countries by 1300, all because doing so was politically useful when conformity was the rule of the day.

In the midst of this thirteenth-century crackdown, Thomas Aquinas, philosopher and priest, argued for the unnaturalness of homosexuality precisely because it didn't occur between animals. Gilles de Corbeil, court physician to the king of France, wrote that "the most ferocious beasts are better than man because they have intercourse and reproduce according to what is in their natural function."

Given that, you can see why witnessing male doodlebugs mating would have given Kelch a crisis. If two male animals can have sex, then it's harder to claim that two male or two female humans having sex are unnatural. The issue wouldn't be going away anytime soon, either: now that entomologists had started looking out for them, more and more accounts of male doodlebug copulations started rolling in.

This caused a crisis at the foremost bug publication at the time, *Entomologische Zeitung*. Anyone who was anyone in the German-speaking bug world subscribed to *Entomologische Zeitung*. The magazine couldn't *not* report on these cockchafing shenanigans. Although it reported news of the male-male copulations, the journal's language went through verbal acrobatics to avoid mentioning the sex of the bugs, saying only that this particular sex act represented "a curious physical form of penetrated parties."

After a heated back-and-forth in the entomology mag, a scientist named Doebner decided to settle once and for all this issue of what he thought was probably mistaken identity: females that amateur entomologists had misidentified as males ("fraglichen Weibchen"). He was bound for a disappointment, though. Once he'd taken a good look at the sets of doodlebug genitalia, he had to confess that he'd found what he called "perfectly

formed, free-hanging male genitalia projecting right outward, pushed out of the way by the insertion of the penis . . . into the anus."

Eventually, someone even drew it up and published a picture of the two males in the act. It's the first known printed image of nonhuman same-sex sex. This position looks *intense*. I assume they worked their way up to it, because I doubt these bugs could have pulled it off on their first go.

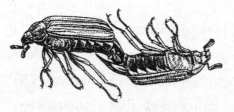

The stakes kept getting higher and higher. If bugs could have homo sex, then it was harder to call homo sex unnatural—which meant there were a lot of people being executed for sodomy that should be, well, alive. (Sodomy criminalization wouldn't be going anywhere soon; it stayed a capital crime in England up until 1861. It remains a life-sentence offense in Uganda—which, by no coincidence, is a former British colony that inherited its penal code from England. Here in the United States, two men were convicted of sodomy in the famous *Bowers v. Hardwick* case as recently as 1986, and the "unnaturalness" of their act was a crucial component of their sentencing. Those sodomy laws stayed on the books until 2003, when Texas judges ruled them unconstitutional . . . citing in their decision the waves of research that had come out in the meantime documenting same-sex sexual activity in the natural world.)

The roots of this ruthless judgment of "unnaturalness" in Western culture are as ancient as the Old Testament in the Bible, in which Adam and Eve enjoyed a pure and innocent existence until their human flaws dragged them down into sin. In the nineteenth century, the big cultural bogeyman in the papers was "decadence" (literally "the fall down"), which was basically all the ways human society had introduced sin into our lives. Nature is pure and good, human civilization is corrupt and evil. Thinkers like Jean-Jacques Rousseau held that we should look to the behavior of animals as our role model. Just look at all those creatures dutifully walking up into Noah's ark in their hetero pairs, after all.

Those animals *had* to be hetero. Otherwise this argument about the "unnaturalness" of same-sex sexual behavior would fall apart.

Truth is, there's always been hand-wringing in the scientific community around the "perversions" of animals. Hyenas had been called out by Greek thinkers as suspect because they were believed to change sex, and a few hundred years later, Isidore of Seville wrote that partridges were suspected of unnatural acts because "male mounts male and blind desire forgets gender."

The roster of immoral animals only gets longer as the centuries pass. Goats came to be seen as promiscuous, and since they had already fallen into sin, some conveniently argued that there was no extra sinning if humans then had sex with them. As a result, it's said that in the sixteenth century the Duke of Nevers brought thousands of goats along with his soldiers into war, to satisfy their sexual needs. We won't look at any pictures of *that* in this book.

So if partridges and hyenas and doodlebugs and—definitely—goats are on the naughty list, where are the upstanding, moral, "natural" animals? Interestingly enough, even though modern zoologists now know that homosexual activity is common in elephants, the Christian theologian Augustine once admired them because he thought they experienced no lust on their own, and had to eat mandrake root as an aphrodisiac in order to be attracted to one another. As scholar Joyce Salisbury frames it, "as they lacked lust, their intercourse approached the ideal described by Augustine for humans: intercourse totally without passion." Sounds awesome.

I think it's no accident that the first case of animal homosexuality to be reported and printed was between insects; it's much harder to accuse a scientist of getting his jollies out of his studies when he's looking at doodlebugs and not, say, sexy goats. When what a scientist is interested in could lead to accusations of the capital offense of sodomy, it's not hard to see why those who observed homosexuality in nature might choose to stick those results in a drawer. The Germans who broke the story of the doodlebugs were either brave or well-connected enough to survive accusations of their own "unnaturalness."

Scientists have historically published accounts of same-sex animal behavior only by shrouding it in the very condemning words that had been used to describe those behaviors in humans: terms like perverse, deviant, and unnatural. In *Biological Exuberance*, Bruce Bagemihl tracks the language historically used around the reporting of same-sex animal behavior:

"Sexual Perversion in Male Beetles" (1896)

"Sexual Inversion in Animals" (1908)

"Disturbances of the Sexual Sense [in Baboons]" (1922)

"Aberrant Sexual Behavior in the South African Ostrich" (1972)

"Abnormal Sexual Behavior of Confined Female Hemichienus auratus syriacus [Long-eared Hedgehogs]*"* (1981)

A 1987 study takes the cake, though. W. J. Tennent published an account of same-sex mating that he titled "A Note on the Apparent Lowering of Moral Standards in the Lepidoptera." Lepidoptera are butterflies. As Bagemihl incredulously put it, "Declining moral standards—in butterflies?!"

While our German entomologists continued to wrestle with what to do about their doodling doodlebug dudes, the uproar spread to France and Russia as well. Noting the reported frequency of male-male copulations in the beetles, another scientist, Carl Robert Osten-Sacken, established once and for all that the doodlebugs weren't raping each other: their sex act was too delicate to be accomplished by force, and he discovered that the larger and stronger doodlebug was often the recipient of the smaller doodlebug's penetration. He still deemed it probably unnatural, but opened the door that it *might* be normal, and therefore not . . . uh-oh. He shied away from the implications: "The interesting philosophical considerations which arise from such abnormal phenomena, I leave to the reader himself to address."

Finally, someone really went there. A later German scientist built on Osten-Sacken's finding that male doodlebugs were both willing participants, arguing that "man-manly mating between insects" is a justification for accepting sexual relations between members of the same sex in all animals—humans included.

The doodlebug torch was taken up one last time by a leading French entomologist, Henri Gadeau de Kerville, who distinguished between doodlebugs who are driven to same-sex sex by lack of females, and those who just . . . like it ("pédérastie par gout"). Even while Oscar Wilde was in prison for his infamous "unnatural" acts of perversion (i.e., having sex with a man), de Kerville called out "certain colleagues who have rebuked me for this paper," before noting that same-sex coupling "is a phenomenon common to the human species and to other animals, including insects, and there are men and women with congenitally homosexual tastes. Why then should we be unwilling to accept the existence of insects which also display congenitally homosexual tendencies?"

He was roundly denounced, including by a leading French physician, who declared that "congenital sexual inversion seems to belong exclusively to man." Keep those animals pure. We humans can have wickedness all to ourselves. Both for reasons of scientific reputations and because of the weight of

tradition that held that "sexual perversion" was a corruption that existed only in the human world, the historical study of same-sex behavior in animals proceeded only in fits and starts. The doodlebug question, picked up time and again by bug fans over the nineteenth century, finally dropped from scientific discourse after de Kerville was so thoroughly scolded by his colleagues.

Interestingly enough, as more research into the sexual behavior of insects has come out, plenty of studies have argued that same-sex copulations in insects might be mostly cases of simply not caring about the partner's sex. Turns out it might not be the easiest thing to figure out whether a doodlebug is male or female, even if you are one. As one study found, being willing to have sex with another creature at the drop of a hat *does* statistically correlate with having more offspring when you're an insect or an arachnid; their philosophy might as well be "have sex with anything that moves in case they'll give you babies." The authors concluded that same-sex behavior "in arthropods is predominantly based on mistaken identification and is probably maintained because the cost of rejecting a valid opportunity to mate with a female is greater than that of mistakenly mating with a male." In other words, why not? You got to have some bug sex, and it's no big loss if it winds up being a dude doodle you just doodled. I'll stop with the doodle puns now.

Another group of scientists independently supported this theory with an ingenious experiment. They placed male beetles in separate containers, with females nearby for some and far away for others, varying how easy or hard it was to find hetero mates. They found that "if searching time for females, and thereby the cost of a rejection error, is experimentally increased, male burying beetles shifted their acceptance threshold and became more permissive." If it's harder to find an opposite-sex mate, better not let any chance for sex pass you by.

The fact is, it's impossible to come up with hard-and-fast rules for animal sexuality. Any article that tries to establish absolute reasons for an animal's partner choice will soon be met by another article disproving it. That isn't a problem for the field—in fact, that's precisely what healthy science looks like. Mysteries and outstanding puzzles are signs that we're interrogating our assumptions, that we're asking uncomfortable and necessary questions. What comes through all these potentially conflicting articles is the diversity of animal sexual behavior. Animals are making individual choices. There is no one way that a doodlebug (or a bonobo, or a penguin) acts. Just like there are no rules for human behavior that don't get contradicted as soon as you make them.

We shouldn't be too surprised that the homophobia of a society winds up embedded in its science. Science is made by scientists, and the way they think about the natural world is reflected in their explanations of it. The "scientific truth" about animal sexuality hinges on whether the writer continues to hold animals as sacredly heterosexual, in what we might call the Noah's ark version of life, or whether they allow themselves to be informed by the undeniable evidence of same-sex sexual behavior.

The history of the scientific study of animal sexuality is a tangled set of contradictory arguments. Depending on who's doing the looking, animals are either perfectly sacred or irredeemably immoral. As sex researcher James Weinrich put it, "If animals do something that we like, we call it natural. If they do what we don't like, we call it 'animalistic.'" Looking into the personal lives of doodlebugs teaches you a fair bit about bug sex, but a whole lot more about human prejudice.

INTERLUDE

WHAT QUEER MEANS

It's hard to name complicated things. It becomes even harder when a topic makes people scared of getting things wrong (like in the cases of race and sexuality and gender and disability), because old terms get shed and new ones rapidly picked up, and people get anxious that they're going to screw up their wording. All too often, that can lead to us avoiding these topics altogether.

I'm going to use some terms in this book that will likely be familiar to everyone ("homosexuality") and some that might not be familiar to some of you ("cisgender"). On top of that, I'll also be using a bunch of terms that are from science, that have developed just to describe queer animal behaviors. There's an additional glossary in the back, but before we get too in-depth, I wanted to do a rundown of how I'm using the most important terms, so we're all on the same page.

Queer: Let's start with the very first word of this book's title. "Queer" is actually one of the oldest labels commonly used to apply to LGBTQIAP+

people, and is an older word than even "homosexual." For centuries, "queer" was used to describe anyone who was considered unconventional, but by the mid-twentieth century it was used primarily to refer to people who were non-conforming in their sexual or gender expression. It was also almost always used insultingly.

By the 1990s, a movement was afoot to reclaim "queer." People who had been called queer in hurtful ways decided to take ownership of the word rather than continue to fight it off. By bravely embracing the term, they argued, they could love away its hurtfulness. Whole academic disciplines of queer history and queer theory formed during this period, based on groundbreaking work like Judith Butler's *Gender Trouble* and David Halperin's *One Hundred Years of Homosexuality*.

Some people don't like using the word *queer* as a stand-in for LGBTQIAP+, because by merging identities into one word, we risk erasing the separate histories of the various identities named (lesbian, gay, bisexual, transgender/transsexual, queer, intersex, asexual, pansexual, and others). Some might be uncomfortable with the term's lingering negative connotations. I totally understand these critiques, but I've still chosen to use queer in this book, because I appreciate the fact that it is language queer people have chosen and is expansive enough a word to also include animal behavior. I do not intend any of its earlier negative connotations, and I hope those who are interested will look into the individual histories of the various strands of queer identity.

Intersex: Refers to someone (human or nonhuman) whose anatomy resists assignment into male or female categories. Biological literature will also use the term "hermaphrodite" to describe nonhuman animals who are intersex, and

I'll continue to do that here for clarity, but that term is outdated for humans and can be considered offensive.

Same-sex sexual behavior: The most commonly used term to refer to homosexual behavior between nonhuman animals in scientific literature. Partly this is because scientists are more comfortable keeping animal sex a separate concept from human sex, and partly it's to avoid words like "gay" or "lesbian," which imply a persistent desire for other animals of the same sex, which for the most part isn't true in the wild. (Spoiler alert: although a few of the animals discussed in this book could be said to have a homosexual orientation, most would more aptly be called bisexual.)

Animal: Humans are animals! That's the kingdom of life we belong to. Technically, if we want to distinguish creatures that belong to Animalia and aren't human, we should say "nonhuman animal" instead of just "animal." That gets clunky quickly, though, so in this book unless stated otherwise I use "animal" to refer to "nonhuman animal."

Sex and Gender: It's often said that sex is a biological definition, and that gender is a social one. That is, sex is assigned based on externally observable genitalia and reproductive system, and gender is determined by your social role. Sometimes the two are one and the same. I'm biologically male and I present socially as male. For some trans people, the two don't agree; someone might be assigned female, but know themselves to be male.

It's tempting to think that because "sex is biological" it's somehow more permanent or definite than gender. As far as the natural world, it's not; most plants are hermaphrodites, and many animal species have both male and female genitalia. Some animals have them simultaneously, and others, like marine snails, begin as one sex and then change sex according to circumstances. The definition of sex that some biologists use is that males have smaller reproductive cells (sperm), and female have larger ones (eggs). That's it.

So. Do animals have gender, or is that just a human thing? Biologist Joan Roughgarden has a useful working definition of gender, which does come in handy when talking about the animal world: she considers it "how an organism presents and carries out a sexual role." Under that definition, animals certainly do have gender. It's particularly useful to keep this definition in mind in chapter 7 about fish—in some species, most of the male fish will be small and look identical to females, while other males of the same species will be larger and different in coloration. Both are males by sex, with similar chromosomes, but have a completely different expression of their sex. We could say that some of those males are gendered female, or represent a gender that is neither male nor female. In chapter 6, we'll also look at mammals who complicate any simple assumptions about gender expression, even under Roughgarden's expansive definition.

Certainly gender expression in animals doesn't play out according to human stereotypes. Female animals are often bigger and more aggressive. Sometimes males give birth and tend the nest. Sometimes it's the females who have the XY chromosomes, and males who have the XX (such as in chickens!). In other animals, males and females appear totally indistinguishable. "Feminine" and "masculine" are human constructs.

CHAPTER TWO: BONOBOS

The bonobo was club president. Of course she was.

Thanks for sharing that, little buddy!

PAT PAT

Hey everyone, what a kick-off, huh?! Welcome to the Gender-Sexuality Alliance. Woo-hoo! Really glad to see you all. Let's introduce ourselves, and I guess, um, I'll go next! Because I'm already talking and everything.

I guess I'm nervous? Which means it's really hard not to be holding hands or grooming you all. But I know we bonobos have a different version of consent than the rest of you, and I don't want to get expelled again and we want everyone to be comfortable so I'll keep my hands to myself.

I mean, you should see Thanksgiving at my house. We all sit down, and before the food's even on the table, we're all having sex, it's totally nuts.

Oh. That's not how it works where you live? Don't get me wrong, it's not a big deal, it just lasts a few seconds and then it's over. Like small talk or something. It only happens because we're all good with it.

So anyway, that's me. Who's next?

BONOBOS

DO WE LEARN HOMOSEXUALITY OR HETEROSEXUALITY —OR JUST UNLEARN BISEXUALITY?

When I was in my early teens, I felt pretty low a lot of the time. Some of that was from being in defend-the-closet mode, worrying that my world would fall apart if the rest of the school decided for sure that I was gay. But it was bigger than that, too. Every day-to-day interaction felt a little meaningless. My mind kept spinning to the big questions: Why are we here? Is it wrong to seek your own happiness when there's so much suffering in the world? Isn't everything we do kind of arbitrary, but it's like everyone's agreed never to acknowledge that fact, so it's sort of like we're all going around lying to ourselves?

Because my brain kept skittering away to these huge questions, the daily things (a math test, going to a football game, celebrating someone's birthday) seemed comparatively meaningless. The storm in my brain couldn't quiet down enough that I could be a real human like everyone else.

If I'd believed in a god, I might have become a hard-core believer, but I just didn't, so that wasn't an option. Instead I tried to find meaning everywhere else. I memorized—actually memorized—all the rules for Advanced Dungeons & Dragons, even though I never found anyone who wanted to play with me. It was strangely comforting to know how many hit dice a displacer beast had. I can still tell you the spells available to a fifth-level cleric. Like other bibles, those rule books gave structure to the world. I was desperate for order. I was desperate for reasons.

As a grade-A nerd (which can hardly be news to you at this point), whenever I was in a slump I'd drag myself into the library and wander the shelves, waiting for one of the book spines to call out, "Here I am, young Eliot, read me for all the answers you seek." I was in the nonfiction section one day when I spied a beautiful coffee-table book called *Thread of Life*. I pulled it off the shelf, figuring I'd distract myself for a few minutes by looking at some cool animal photographs. But the text pulled me in, and I sat where I was and read that book cover to cover, right there on the library's industrial carpeting. When I finished, I smiled for the first time that day. I'd found order, meaning, and purpose, even though I still believed I lived in a universe without a creator.

The topic of the book was evolution, and how the beauty of the natural world came to be through natural selection. I hadn't realized that the sciences could give answers in quite that way: I'd assumed their job was to observe interesting things and to raise important questions, but they couldn't produce the sort of meaning that could give direction to a person's life. I was wrong. Evolution explains *why* life came to be in the form it's in, and what purpose organisms have. Teenage me was one of those things that came to be, so evolution also told me what purpose I had. Boom!

Evolution does nothing less than explain the origins of all of life. Over time, the giraffes that happened to be born with slightly longer necks found they could reach higher leaves—and so they survived to produce offspring that also had slightly longer necks. Then the few of those that happened to be taller than their parents could reach leaves that were even higher, and so thrived over their siblings, passing even longer necks down the line. Over time, the giraffe changed. They are gorgeously suited to their time in the world.

The giraffe's neck came to be for a reason. So did their nose shape, their coloration, the wonder of their eyes and their kidneys, the mineral composition of their hoofs and teeth. Go back billions of years earlier, and single-celled organisms started to cooperate and join together, forming the first multicellular creature—the giraffe's *really* early ancestor. There exists a perfectly logical and compelling explanation for most anything about an organism. The marvelous diversity of life doesn't have to be the work of some magical intelligence; it can result from a force called natural selection, which is as essential to the history of life as gravity is to physics.

My belief that everything was arbitrary and meaningless and empty had left me a lonely and unhappy teenager. Evolution got me out of that hole. It's a little overdramatic to say it saved my life, but it probably got me halfway there.

For example, I'd thought it was incredibly stupid to go to a football game and cheer for our side, when the other team was made up of humans just like us, with their own hopes and worries. Why did we deserve to win more than they did? The evolutionary history of primates taught me how essential in-group/out-group thinking is to our hardwiring, that our tendency to turn strangers into enemies has everything to do with our millions of years spent competing with rivals for scarce resources. The apes who hated the identical apes on the other side of the hill were the ones who chased those "enemies" away or killed them, who survived longer and passed down more of their genes to early humans. Sports reenact that history, only symbolically this time around. (Good luck bringing this up while you're watching the big game, by the way. Trust me, few people want to hear about their monkey brains while they're scarfing down game-day nachos.)

There's no undoing the ingrained emotional appeal of creating "others" and then fighting them. Knowing this, I could cheer our team with a little more passion, because doing so wasn't arbitrary and meaningless anymore. I was fulfilling the destiny written into my primate brain long before I was born. Awareness of this ugly part of our biology can also help us choose when to work against it, to act more kindly and empathetically despite our competitive and exclusionary instincts.

There's a very good reason you are who you are. It's not just random. How wonderful, to be linked into the giant web of life that way.

Our closest animal relatives are the bonobos and the chimpanzees. People often say that we evolved "from them," but that's not really true. We three ape species have a common ancestor, millions of years back, and all of us have been evolving our own ways since then. It's not like bonobos and chimps are locked in time. They've been changing, too. They represent our past only as much as modern England represents the United States' past.

Come meet your nearest relations. Both share almost 99 percent of their DNA with humans, which makes them nearly tied as our closest relatives in the animal kingdom. They look pretty similar, except the bonobo is the one who's smiling.

Trust me, you'd be smiling too if you were a bonobo! While chimpanzees are brutally violent with each other, warring with other groups and even murdering members of their own family, bonobos are known as the "make love, not war" ape. While chimps beat each other up to show who's boss, bonobos will engage in more, um, sensual arts to establish their hierarchy.

Nature documentaries can be a little misleading, because they show you only the most dramatic moments in any animal's life. The perfect day for an ape is a whole lot chiller than it looks on TV: lots of lying about, lots of eating fruit, and lots of farting (trust me, I spent two weeks at a bonobo sanctuary in the Democratic Republic of Congo for research, and bonobo farts are simply epic). On that kind of lazy day, it's hard to see who's boss, because everyone is getting along. If primatologists (people who study apes and monkeys) want to see who's in charge, they'll sometimes introduce a new food to the group. That's when you really get to see who's on top. (And who's a top.)

In a now-famous experiment, a primatologist tried introducing a source of honey to a group of chimps, and then to a group of bonobos. Both sets of apes got *really* excited by the honey. It's their equivalent of candy.

In the group of chimps, the strong young males took control of the honey and beat up any females or elderly males who tried to cut in and get food. This way the tough guys in control remained in control. Everyone else hid away, because the males were riled up by the exciting new treat, and riled-up chimps get aggressive.

When the same experiment was repeated with bonobos, it went very differently. First, they all circled the honey source. They got really tense, showing their teeth and shrieking. You could sense their anxiety: How were they going to distribute this delicious food without fighting over it? The question was overwhelming, so none of them touched any of the honey at first.

That's when, well, they started an orgy. Not just two or three or four of them, either. All the bonobos started having sex with one another. Male with female, female with female, male with male, young and old and everything in between. Some was full-on sexual contact, some was more like what we'd call heavy petting. Bonobos will kiss, too, with wide-open mouths. Only once they were all blissed out did one ape casually take a slurp of honey. Another took some too, then another. Soon they were all sharing the food. Little infants took honey right out of the jaws of big males in their prime, and no one minded. None of them got aggressive, because they were in too good a mood. Friendly physical contact among animals (such as humans!) releases oxytocin, a hormone that promotes bonding. That's why after making out with someone for a few minutes you can feel like you want to call them every hour and write them letters and adopt children someday and get married or at least exchange some bracelets and maybe spend every evening at a table for two at the fancy sushi place in the mall food court. It's not because you've lost your mind—it's because you have oxytocin racing through your brain from all the close physical contact.

Before conflict can get nasty, the bonobos engage in some group sexual activity to get everyone feeling full of love for one another. As a prominent bonobo scholar put it: "The chimpanzee resolves sexual issues with power; the bonobo resolves power issues with sex."

There are only about ten thousand bonobos remaining in the wild, and that small number live only in a hard-to-reach region of the Democratic Republic of Congo, which means it wasn't until relatively recently that anyone studied them. When primatologists finally did start researching bonobos, they found that, yes, they do indeed have a lot of sex, as much as eight times a day.

If two bonobos meet up after a few hours apart, they'll hug and rub against each other for a few seconds, as a way to check in before going about the rest of their day. Bonobo sex can be so quick and casual that primatologists call it the "bonobo handshake." Considering how much baggage sex can take on in our culture, how much built-up expectation we put on it ("do I want it too much? Do I want it too little? Am I doing it right, and with the right person? Should it feel this way?"), and how much judgment and shame ("Am I bad in bed? Am I a slut?"), it's calming to see how unabashedly our close relatives treat it—and what a diversity of sexual acts they'll perform, with no shame whatsoever!

Bonobos will engage in most of the kinds of sex that humans will, from open-mouth kissing up through intercourse. Bonobos will have sex outside of estrus—that is, even when females aren't ovulating and able to conceive offspring. Sex for bonobos doesn't have to be biologically "productive" to be worthwhile.

Low-ranking young bonobos will sometimes mount their older and higher ranking troopmates, showing that "who's on top" doesn't have to be an act of dominance, but instead can be one of play or exploration. Given the judgment or criticism our society can sometimes assign sexual partners in the "submissive" role, whatever their gender, it's a relief to see bonobos receiving one another sexually without setting up an uneven power dynamic. Bonobos will also have sex face-to-face—they are the only animals other than humans that are known to do so.

More important for what we're talking about in this book, though, is that bonobos are bisexual. Throughout their lives, most bonobos will have sexual partners of both sexes. And it's not that they'll just occasionally get together with members of their own sex—homosexual encounters among bonobos are actually *more* common than heterosexual ones.

A few years back, some primatologists spent what must have been a fascinating year logging all the sexual activity of the bonobos they observed and plotting the results into a spreadsheet. (I do wonder what they named the file!) The most common activity? What they called "F-F genito-genital rubbing": females hugging and rubbing their pelvises against each other. When I was conducting my research at Lola ya Bonobo, a sanctuary for orphaned apes in the Democratic Republic of Congo, I often came across females engaging in this very act, and they enjoyed it so noisily  that I blushed and had to walk away to leave them in privacy.

One theory for why bonobos are so promiscuous is that they prevent violence by obscuring family lines. Because they have sex with so many partners, bonobo mothers have no way of knowing who has fathered their offspring. Since no bonobo can be sure about who is a relative, that makes them unlikely to bully anyone else. When someone might be your brother or daughter, you're more likely to treat them well, because they share more of your genes. This prevents aggression especially from males, who in other ape societies can harm and even murder the infants of other males so their own offspring do better in the next generation.

Primatologist Robin Dunbar theorizes that it's the large size of bonobo foraging groups that led them to develop a hypersexual society. Because so many of them are together around food—twenty or more, compared to the five chimps in a typical foraging group—the bonobos had to develop a better means than fighting to defuse food competition.

But as Dunbar notes, it's homosexual sex in particular that lies at the foundation of bonobo society: "If you're looking for homosexual sex in vast quantities, forget humans, it's bonobos you want." By engaging in so many "bonobo handshakes," females feel a rush of oxytocin together, and as a result are highly bonded. This gives them a tight social network. The females are physically smaller, but if a male gets aggressive toward any one of them, she can count on a squad of intimate female allies having her back.

Over millions of years, male bonobos have learned that the females have too much social support for male violence to succeed—and so they've learned to give in instead and enjoy the sexual Olympics. Chimpanzee females don't bond the same way, so the males are able to keep them isolated from one another, making them vulnerable as a result. Ever since they diverged from bonobos roughly two million years ago, chimps came to evolve a patriarchal, hyperviolent society.

Our bonobo cousins provide us with an important lesson: social connection among primates (like us) matters not just for happiness, but for survival. Sex produces oxytocin, and oxytocin bonds us, and those bonds produce a more stable, cooperative society. To put nonscientific words to it, oxytocin bonding looks a lot like what we call love, and the bonobos show that love is a survival strategy. Same-sex love in particular.

They also don't exhibit shame around their sexual lives. They don't judge the partner choices of others. They don't value heterosexual sex over homosexual sex, and in fact for them there's no such thing as exclusive hetero- or homo-sexuality.

The more females in the troop a bonobo has sex with, the more close allies she has. Remember, this animal has almost 99 percent identical DNA to you, and proves that being sexually connected to someone of the same sex or gender is nothing to be ashamed of. In fact, it can be the source of our greatest power.

See what this all means? It means you shouldn't believe it when someone tells you "men are meant to be with women and women are meant to be with men," that it's "Adam and Eve, not Adam and Steve," that heterosexual union is "the way of the natural world." There's nothing more natural than wild apes in the jungle, and these bonobos are as bi as it gets. The famous psychoanalyst Sigmund Freud had a lot of bonkers theories about sexuality, but I do think he might have put his finger on what the narrowing Western culture has done to the diversity of our own sexuality when he argued that maybe we don't go about learning heterosexuality or homosexuality—maybe we actually just forget our bisexuality.

LUCAS DE BREED

Q&A

CHRISTINE WEBB

(EDITED FOR LENGTH AND CLARITY)

NAME: **CHRISTINE WEBB**
PRONOUNS: **SHE/HER**
WEBSITE: **WWW.CEWEBB.COM**
JOB: **PRIMATOLOGIST**

ELIOT: Your recent research concerns how apes express consolation and empathy. Could you tell us more about that?

CHRISTINE: Consolation is when individuals offer comforting, reassuring contact to others in distress. It's a key behavioral marker of empathy. We're learning that stress can actually bring individuals together again, and maybe even in ways that aren't just restorative, but facilitate stronger social bonds. I've never had a close relationship where I didn't have some type of conflict, and it's often through those complex post-conflict interactions that we build relationships in new and important ways. I did my PhD on conflict resolution, and that's when I first learned about post-conflict behavior in apes. Some of the behaviors they use are embracing and kissing, even putting their fingers in the other chimp's mouth. My student recently had a wonderful paper about how, after a young infant died, the chimpanzees consoled the mother who had lost her infant. Reassurance is helpful across many different types of stressful situations.

ELIOT: How does same-sex sexual behavior enter the equation?

CHRISTINE: What was interesting about our paper [on fellatio between male chimpanzees during a socially tense period] was that same-sex behavior in general is something that people often talk about in female bonobos, who have a reputation as the sexy hippie apes.

ELIOT: They have a really good publicist.

CHRISTINE: Ha! Female bonobos are known to engage in genito-genital or "GG" rubbing, but when it came to same-sex sexual interactions we weren't so sure what was going on with chimpanzees. As usual, it turns out that maybe people just weren't looking for it. And perhaps the reputation of chimpanzees as being aggressive belied the possibility that these other types of sociosexual behaviors are going on. The observation of male-male fellatio goes against this orthodox view that chimpanzee males are aggressive with one another and that's it.

And as far as female chimp behavior, what we've always learned in sexual selection theory is that "males compete for females," so we should have known that female choice is really, really important. But the word that gets attached to it is "choosy." Which I really don't like because "choosy" sounds a little bit petty, right?

ELIOT: Yes! Like not being sure if you want boot-cut or regular-fit jeans.

CHRISTINE: Exactly.

ELIOT: I'm curious about the reception for your scientific writing, since it frankly discusses same-sex sexual activity.

CHRISTINE: Our experience was pretty good! If anything, we had reviewers who wanted to push us in directions that I thought were good and important, like asking why we were using the term "same-sex interactions" and not "homosexual interactions." It felt like a safe space in which to explore these topics. The hardest part has been confronting the idea that sexual behaviors always have to have some kind of reproductive function. It reflects the dominant model of evolution that emphasizes selfish competition and the survival of the fittest. But what about cooperation? What about social bonding—which we know is really important for fitness, by the way, right? Social bonds are really important for well-being. Managing conflicts and managing stress and tension are really important for well-being. We've been fixated on one side of the story.

ELIOT: Is that related to how we view animals in general?

CHRISTINE: I think so. We also like to think that humans are special. Anthropomorphism is this word and concept that has been completely weaponized to underestimate and deny the mentality of other beings. One of my favorite concepts is the counterconcept called *anthropodenial.* Biologists want to explain things in the simplest possible psychological terms that they can, but then they come up with all these crazy ideas to avoid ascribing an emotion or motivation to an animal. It's much simpler not to go through all these mental gymnastics to try to find another explanation—maybe other animals are just similar to humans.

ELIOT: You (with Peter Woodford and Elise Huchard) wrote an essay called "The Study That Made Rats Jump for Joy, and Then Killed Them" about how "the gap between knowledge and practice widens when scientists fail to engage with the ethical implications of their own work." I know this is a huge topic and one that's very important to you, but could you introduce us to your ideas here?

CHRISTINE: Sure. It comes down to animal subjectivity and animal moral status. A lot of scientists think that engaging with those ethical issues is going to compromise the integrity of their research, because it would mean that suddenly science is not objective and value-free. Some scientists have an extra incentive to disregard questions around animal ethics, because if they were to seriously and critically engage with those questions, then they couldn't actually do the research that they're doing in the way that they're doing it. If science is considered to be the ultimate arbiter of truth, but is filled with moral contradictions about other animals, then how can we expect society to ever get its act right? Ironically, the science itself would also improve if it took animal subjectivity more seriously.

ELIOT: How do you identify, and how has it influenced your career?

CHRISTINE: I'm a heterosexual cisgender woman. Women are underrepresented in many scientific fields, but not primatology. What I've always found interesting about primatology is there are so many female role models, like Jane Goodall, Dian Fossey. Part of the reason why there are a lot of women in primatology is because you always had these icons to look toward.

ELIOT: What would you like teen readers to consider while they learn science?

CHRISTINE: It comes back to ethical considerations. It's important not just to focus on the group or species level, but to really appreciate the individuality of each animal or plant or other being that one works with. You can form personal, reciprocal relationships with those individuals and relate to them in ways that maybe you're not traditionally trained to as a scientist. Most good scientists that I know don't detach themselves—they engage, and they empathize with the beings that they study, and as a result, they do much better science.

WANT TO LEARN MORE?

Christine is the author (with Jake S. Brooker and Zanna Clay) of "Fellatio among Male Sanctuary-Living Chimpanzees during a Period of Social Tension" in *Behaviour* (2020), which argues that "fellatio between adult males also highlights the apparent behavioural flexibility present in our close relatives."

She is also the author (with Peter Woodford and Elise Huchard) of "The Study That Made Rats Jump for Joy, and Then Killed Them" in *BioEssays* (2020).

Fruit Flies

IS THERE A GENETIC BASIS FOR SAME-SEX ATTRACTION?

I'll be honest: I dragged my feet writing this chapter. Not because there's anything boring about what fruit flies are up to—I mean, we're going to be talking about a "conga line" of insects working hard to make the largest all-male orgy the natural world has ever seen. No, I dragged my feet because talking about sexuality in terms of genes and DNA and inheritance kind of bums me out.

Sexuality is a source of wonder. We're born into life alone, and as we find people we care about and want to spend time with, we have this amazing mechanism of attraction and sensual interaction at our disposal. No one gets to control whom you're attracted to. Those feelings are yours. Of course, culture can be restrictive and can control the ways you feel permitted to *express* your sexuality, but the range of feelings is up to you, and will always have more mystery and subtlety in it than you can ever express. Our main takeaway for sexuality in the animal world, too, is that it will always be more diverse and more expansive than the single story of males and females dutifully procreating that we've been taught in school.

I love that the diversity of human sexuality places us *within* the natural world, rather than setting us apart from it. Queerness is not ours alone. We don't live existences isolated from the ways of bonobos and penguins and, yes, fruit flies. What we experience is experienced by them, too. It's humbling and freeing to know that humans aren't the only creatures with complicated sexual feelings. We're exceptional in some ways, but not all ways. (Exceptional doesn't have to mean better, by the way—sure, we're the only animals to read books. That's cool. We're also the only ones to drop nuclear bombs. And do weird stuff like drink other animals' breast milk.)

I guess I feel like I need to tell you all this because we have to work a little harder to hold on to this sense of wonder in the face of scientific efforts, well-intentioned or otherwise, to identify the genes that "cause" homosexuality. We'll talk about some of the specific developments later in this chapter, but the general thrust is that at various times over the last seventy years or so, some group of scientists or other has established a potential connection between an area of our genome (or our finger lengths, or brain sizes, or fingerprint depth) and same-sex sexual behavior, and then the media has breathlessly run with it until there are cover stories in all the major newspapers and magazines about the fact that the cause of homosexuality has. Finally. Been. Found. Then a few months later, the original study is revealed to be unrepeatable or overstated, and everyone goes back to assuming there's no one genetic trigger for homosexuality after all.

For the most part, the news articles aren't saying anything about what we should *do* with the fact that we now know a supposed cause for homosexuality. But look, there are plenty of things we don't search out causes for, and studies about those things don't make world news. Like heterosexual desire. Where is that produced in the genome? Or blond hair, or right-handedness, or height; where are those coded? Geneticists might be able to provide answers to those questions, but the search isn't urgent in the same way. As historian John Boswell puts it, "What 'causes' homosexuality is an issue of importance only to societies which regard gay people as bizarre or anomalous."

I'd really like for a scientist to finally find an answer to whether rotting fruit tastes better than rotting vegetables, but "nooooo, that's not legitimate sciiiiennce!"

There's an unstated assumption here, that knowing the cause of homosexuality might also mean knowing the "cure." The thing is, queer people have a long history of being viewed as "bizarre or anomalous," both in the culture at large and in the scientific community, and it's led to real and damaging consequences. Homosexuality was considered a disorder in the *DSM* (the chief diagnostic manual in psychology) until 1973. Respected psychotherapists and criminologists in the last half of the twentieth century were still writing nonsense like "it is the consensus of many contemporary psychoanalytic workers that permanent homosexuals, like all perverts, are neurotics," or that "homosexuality, crime, and drug and alcohol abuse appear to be barometers of social stress. . . . Criminals help produce other criminals, drug abusers other drug abusers, and homosexuals other homosexuals."

So say science *were* to identify a "gay gene" in humans (spoiler alert: it has not). What might happen then? What if you spat into a vial and mailed it away to get your DNA results, just because you were hoping to discover you had something cool like Neanderthal DNA, and then you were in a database of "known homosexuals," whether you meant to be or not? (Compiling such a database would take only seconds: 23andMe, one of the biggest sources of commercial DNA-based analysis, participates in studies of gay genes—using [and profiting] from genetic material submitted by consumers, and retaining their genomes in its database.) What if there were a future leader of your country who campaigned on eradicating "immorality," and now had a spreadsheet with "undeniable genetic proof" of precisely who all the homosexuals were? What if expectant parents could go to the doctor in the first trimester of a pregnancy and test for their baby's sexual orientation, with the option to abort the fetus?

These scenarios are dystopian, yes, but that doesn't mean they're far-fetched. While I was inching my way out of the closet in the 1990s, Vice President Dan Quayle was waxing openly on television about how homosexuality was "a wrong choice." The AIDS crisis was in full swing, and otherwise loving people—my hairdresser, my teacher—were talking about how it was a plague that gay men had brought on themselves, finally paying a price for their immorality. "Good riddance" was the unstated—or sometimes explicitly stated—message. In the intervening years, there have been important victories for queer people, resulting from the hard work of activists, including the national legalization of same-sex marriage. There have been setbacks, too: the Trump administration moved to bar transgender service members, and established a so-called Conscience Division in the Department of Health and Human Services that would allow doctors to withhold care—even emergency treatment—to queer folk if a provider claimed it went against their religious beliefs.

Medical interventions have long been used on queer people against their will, from involuntary surgery on intersex people to electroshock treatment administered to "sexual deviants" to "conversion therapy," a psychologically damaging and functionally ineffective attempt to "pray away the gay" in children and teens—that's still legal in most states. Queer sexuality or gender identity was a criterion under the Nazi regime for who was sent to prison or the death camps. After the state created a list of accused homosexuals, an estimated fifty thousand were sent to brutal prisons, and another ten to fifteen thousand were sent to concentration camps, where most died. The yellow star marked Jewish people, and the pink triangle marked queer people. (The pink triangle has since been reclaimed and used as a source of pride, much like the word *queer* itself.)

You can see why it might be dangerous if there were a blood test or saliva test for sexuality. You can see why this is a charged issue for the community.

There's also a way in which, when genetic origins of sexuality and gender identity are discussed, queer people stop being subjects and start becoming objects. As I was doing research for this book, even in contemporary scientific literature I'd run across passages that gave me a bad feeling in the pit of my stomach, passages like:

While homosexuals are more likely to have been effeminate as boys, there are still many homosexual males who have reported more normal childhoods (Phillips and Over, 1992). Weinrich and his colleagues (cited in LeVay, 1994) showed that it is the homosexuals who prefer a more "passive" role (as "insertee") who are more likely to have been effeminate boys.

It took me a while to recognize that I had a bad feeling reading that, and even longer to put words to what the feeling was. Here, the word *homosexuals* is deployed in much the same way as a scientist might discuss deer or fruit flies, some creature to be studied—not "one of us." And who gets to define what makes a "normal childhood"? I know plenty of men who prefer to bottom in sex, but are the "manliest" guys you'll ever meet, according to culturally accepted definitions of masculinity.* And, as anthropologist R. C. Kirkpatrick puts it, "while many self-identified homosexuals recall a gender-atypical childhood, for example, so do many self-identified heterosexuals."

Back to the fruit fly. They're science-famous, the most studied multicellular organisms in genetics, and for good reason. They have short life cycles—about two weeks—and can produce hundreds of offspring a day. If you want to use elephants to study how genes are passed on through generations, you'll have to wait your whole career to accumulate even a couple of data sets. With fruit flies, you can see many generations in a season. They're cheap to maintain in the laboratory—I mean, their dream meal is literally garbage—and there aren't any ethics review boards for drosophila experiments, because no one much cares whether drosophila are suffering (sorry, drosophila).

They also have relatively simple genomes—only eight chromosomes compared to our forty-six—that have been exhaustively studied and mapped already, so beginning an experiment with fruit flies means you can take advantage of an existing mountain of data. Given how different flies appear from us, it can be surprising to learn that 75 percent of the genes that cause disease in humans have equivalents in fruit flies. Their genetics are a simplified version of our own, the way a map is a simplified version of physical terrain—and they're useful for the same reason. If scientists want to go into a creature's genome and start knocking around base pairs to see if they can make some homosexuals, for all the reasons above

---

* I understand there's some discrepancy here, that in the rest of this book I'm calling for animals to be given moral consideration, and then I go and say I hate it when queer humans are discussed like animals. But discussion of genetic triggers for sexuality causes me to start feeling like a bug. I love bugs. But I also don't want to be treated like one. No one ever said that this animal rights stuff wasn't complicated.

fruit flies are a natural first target.

The mid-nineties were a particularly fraught time for queer culture in America. The military had made ignorance official with its "don't ask, don't tell" policy around queer service members; RuPaul's glamazon presence on daytime television was making all sorts of men confused about their supposed heterosexuality; and Ellen DeGeneres's character came out on her sitcom in 1997, which led tons of Americans to clutch their pearls and complain to the FCC that they'd been watching a *gay character on TV*! In the midst of all this, a new study in 1995 led the Associated Press to report that "Researchers Induce Homosexual Behavior in Male Fruit Flies," and then lots of editorials sprang up everywhere about how even invertebrates were getting in on a gay trend.

Two researchers at the National Institutes of Health found that, by manipulating a gene in fruit flies, they could produce males who courted other males. It really turned into a party when they put more and more males together—they all began to court everyone else, and all at the same time. Fruit fly courtship involves what's known as "genital licking," which means—well, maybe I'll just leave that one to your imagination. The important part is that, since it's front-to-back, another fly can get behind the one, then another, then another, until you have an enormous dancing line of male flies, all with their heads in one another's butts. Sexy stuff.

It's frankly amazing, actually. And I don't appreciate your tone.

Aha! This must mean there is a gay gene, yes? Not quite.

There were a number of problems with the study, which ought to have been evident right from the start. The researchers used sloppy language, actually calling the flies "gay," when in fact they were just demonstrating same-sex sexual behavior, not a lasting sexual orientation exclusively to male flies. In fact, the flies *weren't* gay. They were still perfectly willing to engage in courtship behavior (genital licking—last time I'm using that phrase, I promise) with females, if they were available. So if anything, science had discovered a way to make fruit flies express bisexuality. But bi erasure—the tendency for people to focus on the viewpoints of gay men and lesbians, forgetting entirely that bisexual people exist—doesn't just happen at your local queer coffee shop.

Another thing: the scientists also decided to name the gene in question "fruitless," which, well, is a little bit funny but mostly just sucks.

What the NIH researchers had actually done wasn't to turn flies gay; instead they'd removed males' ability to discriminate between male and female fruit flies. That's a far cry from having discovered a "gay gene" in drosophila. It's an even farther cry from establishing there's such a thing as a gay gene in a creature with a genome as complex as ours. But the news sound bites made it seem like we were next, that it would only be a matter of time before we could point to a genetic cause for human homosexuality.

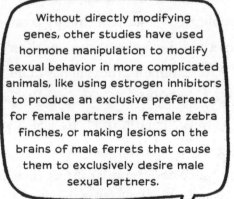

Without directly modifying genes, other studies have used hormone manipulation to modify sexual behavior in more complicated animals, like using estrogen inhibitors to produce an exclusive preference for female partners in female zebra finches, or making lesions on the brains of male ferrets that cause them to exclusively desire male sexual partners.

In any case, as one observer at the time pointed out, "how simplistic it seems to equate genital licking in Drosophila with complex individual and social homosexual behavior in humans." In other words: sexuality in humans can involve a fair bit of genital licking, sure, but also a whole lot more. Sorry, I said "genital licking" again.

Because we can't be studied or modified

as simply as drosophila (i.e., no one's cool with researchers growing us in a lab by the thousands and then playing billiards with our DNA), the sample sizes of human studies are very small—too small to produce results that are conclusive.

That hasn't stopped scientists from trying. In 1991, researcher Simon LeVay published an article in *Science*, one of the world's top journals, claiming that he'd discovered that the region INAH3 of the brain was a different size in gay and straight men. He concluded that, therefore, this region controlled homosexuality. But LeVay had examined only a few dozen subjects, since he was only able to examine the brains of dead people, and those were harder to come by. That's already a very small sample size to use to reach a conclusion, and there was an additional wrinkle in that all the gay men he'd used for the study had died of AIDS; it was unclear whether it was their homosexuality or the disease that had caused the difference in region INAH3 size. A final nail in the coffin of his study was that LeVay's results were never independently replicated. Since replicability is one of the foundations of the modern scientific method, LeVay's conclusions didn't stick.

Research into the genetics of human sexuality made international headlines again in 2000, when the equally prestigious journal *Nature* published studies on finger length, of all things. A study had found that the ratio of the index finger to the ring finger was lower in lesbians than in straight women. Though it didn't find a similar direct correlation in gay versus straight men, it did find that the ratio was low in men with older brothers—which had correlated in previous studies with a greater incidence of homosexuality. (The increased frequency of gayness in younger brothers is thought perhaps to be a result of the changing environment of the mother's womb after each pregnancy—though it could just as easily be from the changing *cultural* environment of a home that has older brothers living in it.)

It's intriguing to think we could discover something about someone's sexuality by examining their hand. Imagine all the "show me your hand" party game shenanigans. Unfortunately, subsequent studies have provided utterly contradictory information about finger ratio and sexuality. It's all just a lot of noise.

The question lurking behind all this is whether same-sex attraction comes from nature (genetics) or nurture (the environment). When scientists want to drill down and really separate how much of a trait comes from nature versus nurture, they turn to twin studies. Identical twins have identical DNA, so if those twins wind up with identical sexualities, even if they were raised in different environments, that's a pretty good sign that sexuality is coded into our genes. If those twins have divergent sexualities, that's a sign that sexuality comes from the environment we're raised in.

The results?

When identical twins are compared to nonidentical twins, the results show that identical twins have sexualities that are slightly more correlated, leading the *New York Times* to conclude "that 50 to 60 percent of sexual orientation might be genetic."

I know. "Fifty to sixty" is the most unsatisfying of percentages. Personally, though, I think that unsatisfying percentages are just what queer people ought to be wishing for. Any more genetic correlation, and we could be in trouble. As the National Organization of Gay and Lesbian Scientists and Technical Professionals phrased it, "On the one hand, we are pleased that there is now scientific support that sexual orientation has an immutable component. On the other hand, this work raises the specter of the various possibilities of screening for such components."

Fruit fly sexuality is probably simpler than ours. But even in their case, the science around specific genes coding for sexual attraction is muddy at best. It only gets harder when we begin to consider the genetics of human sexuality, which has such extraordinary diversity. Even though scientists regularly "simplify" their sexuality research by choosing not to factor in people whose gender doesn't match the one they were assigned at birth (i.e., they habitually erase trans and many intersex people), even then there are still too many variables remaining to allow for any sweeping conclusions.

All genes do is code for proteins. The interplay of those proteins can have elaborate, amazing effects (like producing you!), but genes themselves don't have awareness, intelligence, desires, or goals. They don't have an agenda. It's also increasingly proving impossible to definitively determine how the genetic coding of our DNA interacts with the cultural environments we grow up in to produce individual humans. As Richard Horton put it in the *New York Review of Books*:

The question is: How do genes get you from a biochemical program that instructs cells to make proteins to an unpredictable interplay of behavioral impulses— fantasy, courtship, arousal, sexual selection—that constitutes "sexuality"? The question remains unresolved.

"Unresolved"! Wahoo!

The latest study on the issue, published in *Nature* in 2019, came to a similar conclusion. As its lead author, Andrea Ganna, a geneticist at MIT and Harvard, simply put it: "there is no gay gene."

Sounds good to me.

ANNA CROSBY

Q&A

SIDNEY WOODRUFF

(EDITED FOR LENGTH AND CLARITY)

NAME: **SIDNEY WOODRUFF**
PRONOUNS: **SHE/THEY**
TWITTER: **@WOODRUFFSIDNEY**
JOB: **PHD RESEARCHER**

ELIOT: Have you always been a fan of the wilds?

SIDNEY: I did go outdoors a lot as a kid, but I don't think I was considered "outdoorsy." I grew up in Alabama, and every day after school, I would just go outside and play with my neighbor, who was around the same age as me. We'd walk around the woods, doing random kid stuff: looking under logs, whacking a tree—

ELIOT: Sorry, did you say "whacking a tree"?

SIDNEY: Yeah, you know, like kids do. Destruction all around.

ELIOT: Totally. I whacked a lot of trees when I was a kid. You're bringing back memories.

SIDNEY: No one considered what we were doing "outdoor recreation" or "hiking." When I got to undergrad and found my niche of wildlife sciences, it required a lot of outdoor labs and field trips. I felt detached from it, because I had never gone out deliberately and recreated for the purpose of recreation. I think race has an influence in that, as far as who you see in outdoorsy situations. It's weird: I grew up hiking and exploring the outdoors, but still didn't feel like that was what I was doing compared to what comes to mind when I think of outdoorsy people. So, it's a complicated answer.

ELIOT: When you took your first wildlife and forestry courses, what was it that pulled you in?

SIDNEY: There's always something new to learn outside. Your general understandings of a concept or a species are always changing. I liked being able to learn about something broadly in a classroom and then apply it to the field. The fieldwork component is an amazing part of it all: it makes you feel connected to this broader purpose.

ELIOT: Maybe it's just because I've been doing all these interviews, but I've been wondering lately if queer people are especially drawn to nature.

SIDNEY: There is something there. Once you start to learn about species that don't exist in a binary form, there's this inner feeling of having finally "found your people." When I'm in my classes learning about frogs that can change their sex, it makes me think how there's so much more I have to learn. Let's say you have this preconceived notion of something you see in the wild—you have to change that notion when the creature doesn't behave the way you expect. That doesn't really happen with humans, right? Instead, we try to convince any outlier to fit into the preexisting box. We have to go around convincing each other that this kind of "outlier" human has rights to exist as they are.

ELIOT: In nature, it's okay. You don't have to change.

SIDNEY: Exactly. In my fieldwork [at Yosemite National Park], I've mainly worked with the western pond turtle, a native California species. My work there is mostly about conserving the species. But when I lecture on them, I make sure to bring up that turtles (and some fish groups, and even crocodiles) have temperature-dependent sex determination. The incubation temperature at a particular stage in egg development determines the sex of the individual. It's an evolutionary adaptation, potentially to cope with warming.

When we talked about mate choice in one of my first graduate courses, I remember a lot of us getting very uncomfortable, because the biases or assumptions that we have for humans about sex and gender were put on animals. For example, in the case of salamanders: Some families of salamanders exhibit external fertilization, which means the females put their eggs out into the environment, and then dip out. The male comes along later, uses pheromone sensing to find the eggs and fertilize them, and stays to guard the nests and the eggs. When I teach that in class, my students are always like, "It's so cool! The dad stays and takes care of the offspring!" And I'm like, "Why does that get us all excited?" I get it; male parenting is cool. But we have to remember that what piques our interest also determines what questions we ask and the way we interpret our results. Conclusions can be twisted to form a certain narrative or even move forward in a certain stereotype or tool of oppression.

ELIOT: I love your salamander example, because I hadn't really considered until now that you have to question what brings you joy in the natural world because that, too, can be replicating biases.

SIDNEY: I think sometimes as queer researchers, in our lives, we hope to disprove heteronormative assumptions, but we can also perpetuate those same assumptions within our research. Like I have to keep in mind that if I'm researching sex and wildlife species, I'll want it to be a certain way because of my own gender and sexual identity. It's a lot of power that we have, but in our quest to find inaccuracies in previous research, we have to make sure we're also being humble enough to know that we're not always going to get the answer we want. I want more humility in science.

ELIOT: If you're willing to discuss your identifications, how has their intersection affected your science?

SIDNEY: That could be its own dissertation. I'm Black, biracial, nonbinary, and queer, and that combination has often put me on the margins of whatever space I go into. I've only recently understood what my nonbinary identity means to me, including understanding that it's always changing. It's all made me want to focus on mentoring other scholars like me, so they don't have to go through those same experiences of doubting themselves or feeling on the outskirts. There's a lot of deliberate discussion right now around fighting for diversity and equity and inclusion, which is actually kind of frustrating, because for a lot of racial minorities in these science spaces, our very presence has been doing that fight for our whole lives. I *am* your "diversity statement," the fact that I'm still in this program. I'm not going to sit idle in a system or framework that wants to actively push me out.

ELIOT: You wrote online that "I did not have that moment growing up, looking at Steve Irwin on TV, where I thought that that could be me."

SIDNEY: Yeah, I'm super excited about all these popular Black scientists and science communicators coming up because I can't imagine what position or what space my fellow Black grad students would be in if we'd had our own "Steve Irwin moments" growing up. We are succeeding through a struggle. Imagine if we didn't have that struggle.

WANT TO LEARN MORE?

Sidney is the vice president of MUSE, musementorship.org.

In Sidney's words, "It was started by Mélise Edwards, who identified that need for mentorship from people that look like you and understand your life experiences. There's a lot of institutional knowledge you need in grad school, and I think people who are first-generation and/or historically underrepresented in STEM experience impostor syndrome on a whole different level. I'm now vice president of MUSE and we're super excited that our program is growing. We match people that are interested in going to grad school from underrepresented identities with people that share some of those same identities. We try to make sure students or even mentors know that there is no stupid question."

Bottlenose Dolphins

Are Dolphins Just Gay Sharks?
(Or: Is There True Homosexuality in Animals?)

There's this old TV show called *Glee*. Any theater kids reading this have probably already seen it. I watched it for more seasons than I should have, mainly for one character, Brittany, whose big schtick was to spout these deadpan observations that sounded ridiculous but were actually profound. At one point she says, out of nowhere, "Did you know dolphins are just gay sharks?"

Cut to me, cackling.

That was before I'd done the research for this book, before I even knew about the diversity of sex in the animal world. It just struck me as spot-on about a certain stereotypical kind of gay maleness. Take a shark, give it better skin products, make it more communicative and less bloodthirsty, and you kind of do have a dolphin! (I know not all gay men are like this, but I was willing to go with the stereotyping for the sake of humor.) It also flipped the "gay punch line" dynamic of most media before *Glee*. When being gay is the twist of a joke, it's often in a bummer homophobic way (like "haha, he was actually kissing a *duuuude*!"). Here, it's framed as part of dolphin awesomeness. I mean, who wouldn't rather be a dolphin than a shark? How far can we take this reasoning? Maybe unicorns are just gay horses! (Don't worry, shark fans, I see you, I know you're out there, but you get my point. Also, let's have a moment of sympathy for straight or closeted human males, who don't feel they have permission to express their inner dolphin. Unbloodthirsty straight boys, I see you too.)

Maybe the *Glee* writers' room was full of marine biologists or whale sexologists, who knows. But I suspect they had no idea how close their dolphins-are-gay joke actually comes to the truth. It turns out that dolphins are, well, actually pretty gay.

They're not gay in the way we humans often use the word; most of the dolphins who wind up bonding for life with members of the same sex still also have hetero sex, so technically dolphins are bisexual. But as we're about to see, dolphins are some of the few animals that are like humans in their capacity for long-lasting same-sex sexual orientation. Some male dolphins simply prefer to spend their lives in a sexual union with other male dolphins.

While the most common sexual activity among bonobos is between females (see chapter 2), among dolphins it's between males. When dolphin males get going, they actually put the bonobos to shame. Frisky young dolphin males have sexual contact an average of 2.38 times an hour . . . and the majority of that is with other males. That's forty times the amount of sexual activity that the bonobos have. This all led one newspaper to joke that male dolphins partake "in 'very intense' gay relationships . . . in related news, Grindr has announced a new gay cruising app for dolphins, called Flippr."

There are only two sorts of stable long-term relationships within bottlenose dolphin societies: between mothers and their calves, and between males. Every other relation, including male-female coupling, just sort of comes and goes.

Since dolphins are what's known as "charismatic megafauna"—which means that, like bonobos, the public finds them engaging and wants to buy stuffed animals that look like them—they're easy to get research funds to study, and so there is plenty of great data on dolphin bonding.

We've known for decades that "male friendship" is the main structuring element of the dolphin world. Two or three male dolphins will form an alliance that can last their entire lives. They hunt together, travel together, interact with unfamiliar dolphins together, and mate with females . . . together. Once they've chosen a female they will invite her into the alliance for around a week, mating with her all the while and driving competitor males away. Then the males go their own way and the new mother goes off to rear her calf, often in the company of other females. (Those females will sometimes have sex with one another, too, though not at the same frequency as males do.)

These male couples (or sometimes thruples) bond for life. Those small groups will join others to make an all-male pod of four to fourteen male dolphins who will spend decades traveling the world together. These medium groups will join up with others, making the equivalent of homosexual dolphin empires. They travel the seas, terrorizing the local fish and skirmishing with other dolphin empires, trying to steal their most desirable females. As one prominent dolphin researcher put it, dolphins form "the most complex non-human society on the planet." That society relies on social bonds that are cemented through male-male sex.

Since mothers and calves part ways once the calves are grown, these male bonds are the only truly lasting unit in bottlenose dolphin life. Who knows how we'd define "love" between animals, but if you're willing to ever use the term on a nonhuman, this might be what it looks like. It just happens to be between males. With few exceptions, these males all have sex with females, too. It's just that their significant lifetime attachment—and the majority of their sex—is with males.

What a variety of sex it is, too! Usually researchers in the wild look for what they call "mounting" as a way to add a tick to the sexual activity column of their field journals. But the dolphins are, um, acrobatic, so it's hard to tell exactly who's mounting whom. As one photo caption I came across put it, "the owner of the erection was not identified." Dolphins will mount one another back to belly, back to back, or back to side. They'll also "goose" one another, which involves one placing their beak against the genital area of the recipient and pushing them around . . . which sounds kind of fun? They'll do "push-ups," where one pushes on the genital area of another, lifting them clear out of the water, and they'll stroke or rub one another's genitals with their fins.

The diversity of dolphin sex acts is important, and not just because it represents combinations of male-male, male-female, and female-female. It's also most often nonprocreative. One of the arguments religious conservatives lob at all people, not just queer ones, is that sex is meant to produce children, and any other use of it is immoral and unnatural and ought to make you ashamed. But dolphins, like many of the animals in this book, show that there is a legacy in the

The only way we can do all this acrobatic sex, by the way, is because we have *prehensile penises!* As in, we have muscles to move them, the same way you move your tongue. It helps us grip each other underwater. Trying to have sex with something shaped like a torpedo *without* a prehensile penis—uh uh!

We female dolphins have evolved these labyrinthine vaginas in response, with all sorts of corridors that help us choose which male's sperm actually fertilizes our egg.

natural world of a wide range of usages for sex . . . only one of which is producing offspring. All the creative ways that dolphins mate with one another, including between sexes for which procreation is impossible, prove that sex for reasons other than producing offspring is perfectly natural.

What about the other whales? The truth is, they might have just as frequent occurrences of homosexual sex, but we wouldn't know. Scientists are sketchy on the sex lives of most whales, because their frolicking happens in the privacy of the deeps, far away from our eyes. In fact, for many whale species, even familiar ones like blues and humpbacks, *no* sex of any sort has ever been observed, whether homo- or heterosexual. The only reason we know about same-sex sexual behavior in dolphins and killer whales is because they're the only two kinds of whales that conduct large parts of their lives in the shallows, so they're the only two whom scientists have been able to observe having sex at all. It's intriguing that they both also show significant amounts of same-sex sexual activity. While we don't know what giant blue whales are up to down there, if they're following the trend of their dolphin relatives, then they could be having a whole lot of gay sex, too.

Because male sexual alliances in dolphins are surprisingly similar to how homosexuality has played out in human history, let's see if we can't run what we know about dolphins alongside the history of human male homosexuality to help us understand both a little better.

It turns out that humans didn't have a concept of sexual orientations, either, until relatively recently in our history. "Homosexuality" as a term is actually a fairly modern invention, first appearing in 1891. Before then, there were words in English for the act of when someone had sex with someone of their own gender, but there was no identity attached to it. Throughout the majority of human history and in the majority of human societies, you could have gay sex, but you couldn't *be* gay. It simply wasn't a concept.*

Same with dolphins. I put them early in this book because, of all the animals we're looking at, they form the closest parallel to human sexuality. When people say there are "gay dolphins" they're actually not so far off the mark, as long as they're talking about males. The label isn't a precise fit, though, and not only because most of the males will also have occasional sex with females; many researchers would argue that it's incorrect ever to think of animals as having a sexual orientation, since that implies they see sex as a category in the first place.

It's reasonable to assume that male bottlenose dolphins pursue sex with one another because it feels good. This is a fair assumption because we know that when humans are engaging in similar activities, they're also experiencing pleasure. It's also reasonable to assume that our common ancestor with dolphins evolved to feel pleasure having sex, because sex is important for keeping one's species alive and maintaining a diverse gene pool. The first lucky organisms that began to feel pleasure having sex went on to have more of it, producing more creatures that enjoyed sex, so the drive to find sex pleasurable got stronger over millions of years.

If the majority of dolphin males are going around mating with other males, more than twice an hour, that means dolphins are spending a lot of time having sex that isn't producing any baby dolphins. They could be using all the energy that goes into this acrobatic dolphin sex hunting food instead. That sounds like an evolutionary error, doesn't it? Why would such behavior evolve?

It's a question that's puzzled scientists for a long time, and they have plenty of theories about it. According to dolphin expert Janet Mann at Georgetown

---

* Here's an interesting parallel: It is in the nineteenth century, too, that "vegetarian" became an identity in American and European culture. Before then, one might "follow a Pythagorean diet" in those places and not eat meat, but no one called themselves "a vegetarian." (Yep, one of the earliest proponents of vegetarianism was Pythagoras, the same ancient Greek thinker responsible for the theorem that $a^2+b^2=c^2$ in a right triangle.)

University, the most compelling evolutionary explanation for all this male-male dolphin sex is alliance formation. As we learned from the bonobos, physical intimacy produces social bonding, and sex is as intimate as it gets. These male pairs and trios might have evolved the desire to have sex all the time to keep themselves perfectly loyal and in sync. Then, when they have to hunt together or fight other groups of males, they're more successful. Sex is a social glue.

In many human societies throughout history, males have engaged in homosexual sex for what anthropologists argue are similar reasons: solidifying unions in order to gain social power. Given the recent strides toward greater rights for queer people, it's easy to assume that history has been a smooth glide from fewer rights to more rights, at least as far as the Western world is concerned.

But it hasn't been nearly as simple as that; the increase in rights for queer folk during the second half of the twentieth century was a response to a constriction of rights in the nineteenth century, which saw laws implemented against "unnatural" behavior, including a death-penalty statute in England. That was a reaction to a relatively permissive period after the Renaissance, which followed a surge in antigay legislation in the thirteenth century. It's been an up-and-down ride for us.

If we zoom out to look at human civilization as a whole, though, we find it's for the most part been tolerant and even supportive of same-sex sexual behavior. One significant historical study of all known human societies throughout history found that 64 percent sanctioned or embraced same-sex sexual behavior. Especially substantial numbers of homosexual relationships are found in seventeenth-century feudal Japan, the Mayan civilization, fifteenth-century Florence, and the Indigenous peoples of North and South America. Of course we should add to that list the ancient Greeks, the best known example of idealized male-male love, at least as far as white European culture is involved.

It can be hard for us in the twenty-first century to get our heads around how prevalent and socially acceptable male homosexuality was in Greece. To be attracted to other men wasn't a source of stigma—it was the reverse, a sign of healthy masculinity. In fact, people looked at men who *didn't* enjoy sex with other men as suspiciously effeminate, because they seemed drawn toward the female inside of them. (Which, yes, meant this particular form of pride in male homosexuality came along with a heaping dose of sexism against women!) Greek heroes like Achilles and Heracles had same-sex exploits, as did Zeus himself, and were all considered more manly because they were so drawn to men.

As Plato wrote, "they who . . . hang about men and embrace them, and they are themselves the best of boys and youths, because they have the most manly nature." The general Pammenes, as reported by Plutarch, put a less poetic point on it:

Homer's Nestor was not well skilled in ordering an army when he advised the Greeks to rank tribe and tribe . . . he should have joined lovers and their beloved. For men of the same tribe little value one another when dangers press; but a band cemented by friendship grounded upon love is never to be broken.

Rawr! Tough Warrior Dude Lovemaking! Since there was no concept of "being" gay in ancient Greece, there were only gay acts; during sex one man was the sexually dominant erastes and the other the sexually passive eromenos, and those roles could change as easily as shifting positions. (As they grew older, men would generally go from passive eromenos to active erastes. As Diogenes Laërtius wrote about the desirable Alcibiades, an Athenian general, "in his adolescence he drew away the husbands from their wives, and as a young man the wives from their husbands.")

These romantic relationships between men weren't just about sex. They also produced advantageous bonds. When men came together from wealthy families, it was the result of lengthy courtship and parental discussions to make sure that this sexual union was noble love, not just sex. It was to be a stable and important connection in the men's lives—and a source of political advantage. Since this relationship didn't mean that the men were identifying as exclusively homosexual, the older man could keep his relationship with his wife, and the younger man could go on to marry a woman, and even choose a young man as his sexual partner once he was older and established.

In a culture in which families are vying for social power, each male child effectively had three potentially advantageous matches to make: his early-in-life bonding to a powerful older man, his marriage to a woman from a suitable family, and then his choice of a younger man to be his romantic partner later on. According to his desires, he could prioritize or deprioritize the hetero- or homosexual relationships in his life. All men would be assumed to be some form of bisexual.

Maybe you're as frustrated as I am that there is so little discussion of female sexuality in anthropology. There's a sexist double whammy at play here. Though much has changed in recent years, anthropology has classically been dominated by male scholars, studying the behavior of men. Even when researchers actively seek out the stories of women to complete our picture of the past, they are often blocked; because men were more often the heads of household, were more often the ones making economic choices, were more often the ones receiving educations and writing their stories or the stories of other men, it's much harder to find evidence in the historical records of how women lived their lives. In the case of the ancient Greeks, for example, we know that Sappho wrote love poems to other women and girls on the island of Lesbos (which is the origin of our term "lesbian"!). There is evidence that the Spartans also supported sexual relationships between women, with a similar mentor-trainee dynamic. There's even an ancient Greek device developed for the purposes of sexual play between women—the "olisbo," a leather dildo. But as far as women in general in ancient Greece, or other ancient societies, the historical record is sparse. That doesn't mean it wasn't happening, however! We'll explore the issue of the limited reporting of female animal sexuality more in the next chapter.*

How amazing that the bottlenose dolphins, who have groups of males forming larger and larger alliances and engaging in conflict with other dolphin kingdoms, also evolved a system of male sexual alliances to keep it all glued together. Our human and nonhuman cultures converged, coming up with similar strategies to fill similar needs.

---

* A similar issue comes up in trying to reconstruct the lives of the poor. As they had little access to land and property, the poor left fewer entries in the historical record, and were less often the subjects of painting and literature. Much of what we know of the history of sexuality therefore favors the histories of the wealthy. It's very reasonable to assume that the lives of poorer Greeks were marked by coercion and prostitution more than the culturally sanctioned "noble unions" wealthy Greeks could count on. It's a topic of scholarly debate, as well, as to how young the younger male sexual partner might have been in ancient Greece. Certainly the Greeks had a lower age cutoff than we do for what they considered an appropriate relationship partner. The significant age gap in these male-male sexual unions, even though less controversial in the time of the Greeks than now, would have especially opened boys who weren't from well-connected families to risks of exploitation and nonconsensual sex.

Male alliances as a result of widespread bisexuality make a compelling explanation for homosexual behavior, since they have a lot of upsides for individuals, and few downsides. As anthropologist R. C. Kirkpatrick put it, "in terms of natural selection, homosexual behavior is a benign trait in most instances and becomes adaptive within certain social contexts." Our modern Western tendency to erase bisexuality from our thinking inhibits our understanding of how nonhetero sexuality can be useful for individual animals (both human and nonhuman), and therefore would have naturally evolved over time. Sex with people of the same sex would only be an evolutionary roadblock if it meant you never had sex with those of the opposite sex.

But if dolphins and humans are some version of bisexual, then they still pass on their genetic code, and so they're not an evolutionary dead end, not at all—and they get to enjoy the social benefits and pleasures that come with a wider range of sexual activity.

CHAPTER FIVE: JAPANESE MACAQUES

Normally I don't have to do this myself. Madison or Isabel or Emma does it. But they're not in this club, so . . .

I mean, it's fine. I can groom myself. It's just better when they do it. I know you all wish you could sit with us in the cafeteria, but I'm sorry, it's a very select crowd and there are only so many seats at that table so we have to make choices.

You know you ladies are just doing that grooming and kissing and stuff to show off for all the boy macaques.

Excuse me?! Who do you think you are, talking to me like that? Have you EVER seen a boy sitting with us? We barely ever have sex with boys, it's mostly just us girls. Ugh!

Sheesh! Sorry!

Now you're *definitely* not sitting with us.

JAPANESE MACAQUES

WHERE ARE ALL MY LADIES AT?

There are lots of female animals in this book. But those examples took some digging. Unfortunately, it's much easier to find research on the sex lives of male animals.

Once observers are looking for it, they discover plenty of female-female sexual activity in the animal kingdom. But there's no denying that as a whole science tends not to focus on female animals. Think about the peacock, or other birds with extravagant displays of color in their plumage. We learn to admire the lengths a male goes to for a chance at a female, the iridescent colors he'll display, the ritualized dances he'll learn, the grave risks he'll take, all to dazzle a female who submits to his performance and allows him to be the father of her chicks.

It used to be thought that sexual selection—the term for when mate choice modifies a species over a time, regardless of how it might impact their survival rates—was another way of driving the fitness of a species. Females desire males that will pass the healthiest genes to their offspring, the thinking goes, and a male has to be doing exceptionally well to be able to afford to produce those ridiculous giant feathers. Scientists assumed that females were knocked off their feet by all that swagger. "Wow, for that male to afford a sports car like that, he must have tons of resources. Come over here, big boy."

That's the story we tell ourselves about the peacock. But what of the peahen? In that story of the peacock, we could just as easily place the female in the driver's seat. She chooses, and she's shrewd in her choices, and over millions of years males have been changing their bodies according to her whims. A male peacock's feathers are beautiful, yes, but they also make him unfit for survival, rendering him easily visible and eaten. But she's decided she wants just this shade of emerald green in her men, that she wants the tips of his feathers

Wait, you're telling me that other birds are *into* that?!

to look like groovy blue eyeballs. The males that peahens prefer are the ones who get to pass their genes along to the next generation, which means that that next generation will have more males with even more outlandish feathers. He's evolving to suit her, and she's selecting only the males who submit to her will. She is the author of his change.

Maybe females aren't choosing the bluest or the shiniest or the prettiest males because their beauty is a symbol of their fitness. Maybe they're choosing them simply because those females *like* things that are blue or shiny or pretty. The quality they're seeking could be fairly random, and not tied to fitness at all. They might be basically testing males, saying, "I'm only going to go out with guys who realize what I like, and who work to produce it." The point isn't the steps the male is dancing, but the fact that he's learned the steps. Females could have been choosing males time and again who are attentive to them, evolutionarily speaking, passing over self-centered or inattentive males.

We might have been wrong about the story of the peacock. It's not males outdoing one another to dazzle females. It's females training males to cater to female desires.

Though more women are in science than ever before, it's long been dominated by men. Men in the field, men teaching the college classes, men writing the textbooks. My textbook in high school was called *Biological Sciences*, and there's a good chance it's the one you're familiar with, too. In it (and in health class, for that matter) I learned a "Sleeping Beauty" version of fertilization. The egg was unmoving, while a squadron of energetic sperm sallied forth into foreign territory, meeting untimely ends left and right until one hero reached the egg and busted his way in. Or, as my textbook put it:

Conditions in the vagina are very inhospitable to sperm, and vast numbers are killed before they have a chance to pass into the cervix. Millions of others die or become infertile in the uterus or oviducts, and millions more go up the wrong oviduct or never find their way into an oviduct at all. The journey to the upper portion of the oviducts is an extremely long and hazardous one for objects so tiny.

Sperm as hero; egg as virgin land to be conquered, full of great danger and great reward. These are the stories men like to tell ourselves. As the gender historically with more power, we've also made these hero's journeys the base of white European and North American culture. *The Odyssey*, *The Lord of the Rings*, *Star Wars*, the Harry Potter series: a (classically male) figure receives a call to adventure, goes on a journey, encounters hardships, gets the girl, is the special one to triumph and change the world.

Here's the trickiest part: because we love these stories, we tell them to ourselves over and over, so they reinforce one another until we're convinced they're how the world works. The same is true for scientists. When they encounter a fresh situation—like observing a group of monkeys—they don't arrive with a clean slate. They will have unavoidable intuitions based on how they understand the world to operate. Ideally those biases can be questioned, challenged, or altered, but there's no avoiding that initial intuition. And our intuitions, formed in childhood, are that males are agents, that they are sexual pursuers, and that females are receivers, and that they will "submit" to males. I've read many scientific articles in order to write this book, and I can't tell you how often it's said that a female will finally "submit to" a winning male. Mentions of the possibility of female sexual desire are rare.

The problem with the sperm story above is that it's not true. Once it became accepted as the truth, though, that prevented scientists from reconsidering the situation. It turns out that the egg is not the passive land through which the heroic sperm wanders. It is more like a domineering coach, telling the spermies where to go, how fast to move, and finally choosing a winner. All along, there have been microvilli on the exterior of the egg.

Mammal sperm can't fertilize an egg without effectively getting permission first; the egg secretes enzymes that activate the winning sperm, a process called capacitation. Then, once the sperm reaches the ovum, it releases enzymes against the egg, a sort of knock on the door. They can't break down the wall, though, until the egg releases more secretions that activate those enzymes for that sperm. Then the microvilli clasp the sperm and guide it in. As the scholars who authored an article on the topic for *The Sciences* put it, "Ever since the invention of the light microscope, researchers have marveled at the energy and endurance of the sperm in its journey to the egg. Now, with the aid of the electron microscope, we can wonder equally at the speed and enterprise of the egg, as it clasps the sperm and guides its nucleus to the center." The egg isn't a prize to be gained; fertilization is a two-way conversation, with female choice playing a much larger role than most of us have been taught.*

We have a long way to go to undo our assumptions around sexuality: namely, that men are active, and that as far as females are concerned, their sexuality is reactive to males, and tied primarily to reproduction. Thankfully, our primate relatives give us some great counterexamples. We've already looked at bonobos

(chapter 2). Now, enter the Japanese macaque monkeys.

If I get reincarnated, I want to be a Japanese macaque. Commonly known as snow monkeys, they are the primates who live farthest north, throughout the Japanese archipelago. The reason they can live even in snowy and cold climates is that they take over naturally occurring hot mineral baths. If you want to have a really fun

afternoon, look up videos of "snow monkeys in hot baths" online. They perch at the edge like professional bathers, snowflakes gathering on their eyebrows as they soak their furry bodies in steaming water.

Because a lot of their time is spent in close quarters, with limited access to prime bathing positions, snow monkeys have to do a lot of negotiating. One of

---

* Just to be totally clear—this happens on the cellular level, not the brain one! There is no evidence that any amount of conscious thinking about whether a pregnancy is desirable will alter what happens on the level of the sperm and egg.

> If everyone wants to pat your hair and make sure you have no parasites, it's a pretty good sign that you're one of the cool kids.

the ways monkeys negotiate is by grooming, using the visible proof of who's grooming whom to send messages about which monkey is on top of the hierarchy.

Another way they negotiate is through sex.

It's long been known that there's a lot of female-female sex between macaques. In other varieties of the monkeys, like the rhesus macaques, experts have concluded that homosexual sex evolved because it results in alliance formation. It's a theory similar to the bonobos, or to the bottlenose dolphins (chapters 2 and 4); sex releases oxytocin, which promotes bonding. It is also a visible, public demonstration of goodwill between two females, which serves a similar function as grooming. Together, they work as political moves within the troop's structure.

In the case of the snow monkeys, though, the purpose of all this female-female sex isn't so clear. This has led primatologists to caution that there might not be a blanket homosexual behavior common to macaques, but rather plural homosexual behaviors. Monkeys and apes have cultural variations just like humans do. Just as homosexual behavior looks different in Iran than in Canada, so too does it differ between monkey populations.

> Don't even start with me about the Shikoku macaques.

Sex between female macaques isn't all that different from sex between males and females.

One female mounts another, and both "exhibit a reddening of the face and perineum that is associated with increased receptivity and proceptivity." In other words, they both appear to be enjoying it. Quite a bit.

For decades, scientists who observed same-sex sexual behavior in the field would avoid calling it sex, explaining it away as a social interaction that is something else entirely. As one scientist described same-sex mounting in lions, "it's a social interaction that has nothing to do with sexual pleasure."

In one of the few experiments of its kind, primatologist Paul Vasey and his laboratory set out to examine the various possible motives for the frequent female-female sex in snow monkeys. They recorded all the sexual activity for a captive population of the monkeys and tested each of the various hypotheses that have been proposed for the purpose of all this female-female sex.

Dominance Demonstration

Theory: Perhaps sexual activity is a way for one animal to express their social dominance over another. (This is the most frequent theory used to explain away same-sex sexual behavior in animals.)

Conclusion: Unsupported by evidence. Initial sexual roles (mounter and mountee) in an encounter don't correlate with status in the dominance hierarchy. Furthermore, sexual encounters between females are "bidirectional," meaning both females will take turns mounting and being mounted.

Acquisition of Male Mates

Theory: Maybe this is all to get a guy! Females stage sexual encounters to excite nearby males. They're not really into one another, they just pretend to be for male pleasure. (I'd call this one the "you wish, guys" theory of monkey lesbianism.)

Conclusion: Unsupported by evidence. This theory falls apart on three counts. It would predict that 1) females only have sex in front of males, 2) female-female mounting would occur only when a female is fertile and able to conceive, and 3) female-female mounting would stop once a male becomes involved. Vasey's study showed that none of these predictions hold.

Acquisition of Parental Care

Theory: By having sex with other females, females create a partnership that helps them care for their own offspring. (Note this theory shares some resemblances with the "same-sex households" that have been demonstrated in gulls, albatross, and ducks (chapter 8).

Conclusion: Unsupported by evidence. None of the females who had sex with other females expressed care toward the other female's offspring. In fact, they were more like uncaring or even hostile: in 10.5 percent of conflicts, the females actively worked *against* their lover's children. Sort of a wicked stepmother thing going on.

Reconciliation

Theory: Like it is for the bonobos, sexual activity in snow monkeys is a way to reduce tension following conflict. Female-female mounting is a convenient way to smooth over upset feelings after a fight.

Conclusion: Unsupported by evidence. Vasey found that female-female sexual activity in snow monkeys didn't cluster in postconflict times. In fact, "subordinate consort partners were more likely to perform same-sex sexual solicitations and mounts before an aggressive interaction than after."

This led Vasey to a startling conclusion: "Despite over 40 years of intensive research on this species, there is not a single study demonstrating any adaptive value for female-female sexual behaviour in Japanese macaques." In other words, there isn't an evolutionary benefit to it. Females are having sex with females because it feels good, and because they want to.

It's a surprisingly controversial take, since it's deeply ingrained in how we talk about animals to think about them as instruments serving ends, not as beings who have their own feelings and desires. When we *do* talk about animal sexual desires, it's generally male desire that gets discussed.

Oh, I am **HERE** for this.

Of course, Vasey's not just establishing that macaque females experience desire, which is already a provocative idea. He's also arguing that females experience desire for *one another*. This flies in the face of another trend that inhibits the writing about female sexuality in animals: we have a broad biological definition of sex when it comes to heterosexual behavior, and a narrow one when it comes to homosexual behavior. This is true across species lines. As philosopher of science Vinciane Despret put it, "When I was a student, we learned in an ethology course that when an ape presents his or her genitalia to another and allows himself or herself to be 'mounted'—I also heard this said of cows—it has nothing sexual about it; it is just a way of affirming dominance or submission, depending on the position adopted." Or, even more strikingly, in Bruce Bagemihl's *Biological Exuberance*:

> *When a male Giraffe sniffs a female's rear end—without any mounting, erection, penetration, or ejaculation—he is described as being sexually interested in her and his behavior is classified as primarily, if not exclusively, sexual. Yet when a male Giraffe sniffs another male's genitals, mounts him with an erect penis, and ejaculates—then he is engaging in "aggressive" or "dominance" behavior, and his actions are considered to be, at most, only secondarily or superficially sexual.*

Vasey isn't arguing that female snow monkeys are having sex by accident. The female macaques derive pleasure from sexual stimulation, because desiring sex has been good for the species as a whole, including during its long history of male-female sexual interactions. If the desire and equipment are there, it shouldn't be surprising that female macaques take advantage of sexual good feeling by also enjoying it in same-sex pairings. It doesn't need an explanation like "showing another female who's boss" or "turning on the guys." It can just be about female pleasure, as simple as that. But, as it has been in the fields of history (Catherine the Great) and literature (*The Scarlet Letter*) and music (Cardi B's "WAP"), female pleasure is controversial.

In humans, famed analyst Sigmund Freud was one of the first to publicly acknowledge even the possibility that females experience sexual pleasure; previously, the thought was too scandalous in European culture even to be entertained. Although he was brave enough to bring it up, Freud then went to great lengths to explain it away, arguing that women's experience of sex is rooted in the fact that they are jealous of men's penises, and use sex as a way to temporarily possess one.

Wait, *what* did he say?!

Even though he was frank about his inability to give female sexuality its full due ("That is all I have to say to you about femininity . . . it is certainly incomplete and fragmentary and does not always sound friendly"), Freud did ask his readers to leave the door open for science to propose broader ways of thinking about sexual desire in women. "If you want to know more about femininity, enquire about your own experiences of life, or turn to poets, or wait until science can give you deeper and more coherent information."

Science has come a long way from its male-focused roots, but there is plenty more work to be done. Female agency and desire are important mechanisms in the animal world, from the active choices made by the ovum itself through the power of the peahen in directing the evolution of the peacock. It's perfectly reasonable that female choice and female desire might result in sexual unions that don't involve males at all! As anthropologist Linda Wolfe put it, female-female sex "is just part of what they do, socially and to derive pleasure. It is probably mostly just for sexual pleasure."

How simple and how freeing—and how important—that the most compelling reason for why female macaques engage in sex with one another is also the simplest: pleasure.

You still can't sit with us at lunch.

Q&A

MOUNICA KOTA

(EDITED FOR LENGTH AND CLARITY)

NAME: **MOUNICA KOTA**
PRONOUNS: **SHE/HER**
WEBSITE: **WWW.MOUNICAKOTA.COM**
JOB: **EVOLUTIONARY BIOLOGIST**

ELIOT: What's been your journey as a scientist and a researcher?

MOUNICA: You know, I wasn't much into science at all as a kid, actually. I had a really big interest in communication. Part of that was because I had issues of my own communicating; I was struggling with queer identity and not being able to come out. Taking an animal behavior class, I started learning more about the ways that communication evolves within animals. I thought, "Oh, well, this is the subject for me!"

ELIOT: You study sexual signaling. What does that mean?

MOUNICA: Sexual signals are methods of communication typically used by male animals to attract female potential mates. They come in a lot of different modalities, like elaborate dances or vibrant colors. I work with crickets; their way of sexually signaling is through singing extravagant songs. Anytime you hear crickets singing in the afternoon, that's males trying to court females. But predators or parasitoids will also be attracted to them, so they run the risk of dying anytime they do it.

ELIOT: How does female choice play into sexual signaling research?

MOUNICA: Female choice is emerging as one of the biggest questions in evolutionary biology, especially sexual selection research. When Darwin first proposed the idea of sexual selection, he kind of wrote [female choice] off as a simple aesthetic preference, like preference for a color. But really, there are several reasons why female choice could have evolved, usually because females search for high-quality mates, so their offspring have a better chance of survival.

ELIOT: How would you describe the response to your work?

MOUNICA: Stereotypes bleed into the way that we "objectively" do science. For a long time people didn't think that females ever initiated sex in the animal kingdom. Or, take the case of same-sex sexual behavior: a lot of the time they would just assume they were seeing male-female coupling, but it may not have been. If the organisms aren't dimorphic, they don't have noticeable characteristics that help human observers identify their sex. They would just assume they were seeing different-sex sexual behaviors. We like to think we derive a lot of our ideas from the animal world, but it's actually the opposite; we put a lot of our ideas onto the animal world.

Like take the Laysan albatross (see chapter 8). Why do they have these female-female pair bonds and raise chicks together? All the hypotheses revolve around males—that it's male scarcity, right? But what if we centered the females; why would their behavior evolve adaptively? I love the Laysan albatrosses, by the way. They're like my lesbian moms. I have a big photograph of them in my office.

ELIOT: If you're willing to discuss your identifications, how have they influenced your career?

MOUNICA: I identify as a lesbian and a woman. I was born in India, but we immigrated here when I was two, so most of my life has been in America. Early on in my childhood I didn't have much in the way of role models of color, but at the same time I know I'm an upper-caste Indian, so I'm trying to be very conscious of the fact that I have that privilege; I'm afforded a lot of opportunities oppressed-caste people aren't. It's a trade-off, because I also grew up in a very white area of Texas. It didn't actually feel like I could do science, and I still feel, a lot of the time, like I'm infiltrating a space that's predominantly white. In grad school as well, all the professors in my department were white. In my current department, I've made a lot of really good friends of color. A lot of my coworkers are queer, too.

There's this really beautiful quote by Elizabeth Rush,[*] that science is this

---

[*] "But just as paying attention to another person fosters intimacy and makes us feel less alone, perhaps scientific observation allows us to enter into a similar relationship across species. By listening, by returning to the grove time and again, by tuning our ears to the sounds of beings unlike ourselves, we begin to reenter what Thomas Berry, the Catholic eco-theologian, calls 'the great conversation' between humans and other forms of life. This too can have a grounding effect, can help stave off a different, larger, and more gaping loneliness. If anything is sacred, it is this, I think. And by this I mean all of it: the salmonberries beginning to ripen in the bramble; the scratchy, scolding caw of the Steller's jay that will nibble there; the long, straight trunks of the Pacific red cedars that rise into the sky's blue cathedral. The web of life that too often capitalism seems dead set on dismantling." Elizabeth Rush, *Rising*, 199.

conversation between humans and other types of beings. We have great diversity of other beings, but if we have a very homogenous human voice speaking, that doesn't make for a great conversation.

ELIOT: Is there anything you would like to tell young people considering a career in science?

MOUNICA: I'm very defensive of kids. I grew up as a kid who was not taken care of, so when I go into classrooms my primary purpose is to validate the hell out of whatever their ideas are.

ELIOT: Validate the hell out of their ideas. That's great.

MOUNICA: They have the capacity to be a scientist. Everyone is a scientist, by merely asking questions about the world around them. They're powerful enough to ask questions and have valid perspectives on the world.

WANT TO LEARN MORE?

Mounica is the author (with Ellen Urquhart and Marlene Zuk) of "M. Spermatophore Retention May Accommodate Sexual Signal Loss in Pacific Field Crickets" in *Behavioral Ecology and Sociobiology* (2020), which "investigated how two components of female mate choice are involved in rapid sexual signal loss in the Pacific field cricket (*Teleogryllus oceanicus*)."

In this video, Mounica introduces general audiences to her research—with a special guest appearance by her veiled chameleon, Juno, and bearded dragon, Morgana! marketsci .org/2020/08/01/mounica-kota-invertebrates

EER

ARE THERE TRANS ANIMALS?

When I was in elementary school, I had a long bus ride home each day. It took over an hour, but I didn't mind in the least; I was a quiet kid, and after a noisy school day I enjoyed pressing my forehead against the window and staring out at the rural California countryside.

I remember the moment when, as I was staring out a rainy windowpane after an hour of daydreaming, I watched kids get off the bus and realized that I had no way of knowing that they were like me inside, no way of knowing whether they had consciousnesses of their own. They could be robots or aliens! How could anyone know?

Short answer is that we can't, no matter how hard we think about it. It's the stuff of science fiction plots, but it's also a real problem for ethologists, the scientists who study animal behavior. It's hard to verify any other creature's internal experience of the world, even when that creature is another human— and it's especially hard when we start thinking about nonhumans. This puzzle is known as the "other minds" problem, and it's really done a number on what scientists are "allowed" to theorize about animals.

Nobel Prize–winning ornithologist Konrad Lorenz observed how similar a greylag goose whose partner has died behaves to a human who is grieving: "the musculature becomes limp, the eyes sink deep into their sockets, and the individual has an overall drooping appearance, literally letting the head hang." He goes on to note that it's only when describing humans, however, that a scientist can attach the word *grief* to the underlying mental state. Naming emotions in animals is not classically considered rigorous science. (For more on this long trend in the sciences to deny that animals have feelings on the scale of human feelings, see Christine Webb's Q&A on page 40.)

Around the time I was on that school bus in California, I started to realize that I wasn't like other boys. But how could I tell people about all the things I was feeling, and have them believe me?

The "other minds" problem is a roadblock in trying to get acceptance for queer people. I'm a gay man. I *know* that I'm gay. Therefore, it's very reasonable for me to assume that other people can be gay. But I'm also cisgender, meaning my gender expression is the same as the one that I've always lived with. Since I'm not trans, I haven't felt the experience of my lived reality not matching the sex assigned to me at birth. Since it's not *my* experience of the world, and I therefore don't have any direct evidence of what being trans feels like, if I were the suspicious or mean sort, I could claim that being trans is all some sort of hoax.

Heck, a lot of people who identify as 100 percent gay or lesbian need convincing that *bisexuality* really exists, claiming that bisexual people are "just in a phase" or "haven't fully come out yet." (Which makes me chuckle researching this book, as it becomes increasingly clear that bisexuality came earlier in the history of life than homo- or heterosexuality, and people who identify as 100 percent gay or lesbian or straight are likely to be underestimating their *own* bisexuality.)

One wonderful thing about being a human is that we can describe our internal states to one another through language. It's what's happening right now, as I write down my thoughts and you read them. Therefore, when we meet you can tell me your experience of your gender, that your pronouns are they/them, or that you don't feel like you fit any gender today, this year, or ever. Or that, although you are read as male, you are a woman. I love the wealth of identities that have come up around gender expression; new phrases can help us both figure out who we are and communicate our complicated selves to others.

Terms like nonbinary and cis and trans convey a gender identity and can be combined with other sets of terms to communicate who we are or aren't attracted to, words like demisexual or asexual or fluid. A crucial element of understanding a modern human's gender identity or sexual orientation is their verbal communication of it. You most likely have met people you knew were trans, and then you might have met others that you wouldn't have realized were trans until they decided to discuss it with you.

Combined with the "other minds" problem, this makes it difficult to talk about gender expression or sexual desire in animals. A person could be bisexual, attracted to two or more genders, but never have acted on their desires; without the benefit of language, an outside observer would have no way of knowing that person's bisexuality. The same goes for animals; we have very little way of knowing whom they're attracted to without evidence—i.e., sexual behavior. Similarly, it's impossible to know a nonhuman's internal experience of their own sexual identity. So, for the most part we'll have to leave the question open as to whether animals might have a more complicated gender or sexual identity than external observation allows for.

To answer this chapter's guiding question early: No, we can't say for sure that there are trans animals. Without language, there isn't anything in the animal world that neatly corresponds to the human experience of being trans or nonbinary.

What we *can* identify plenty of in the animal world are animals that live outside of sexual binaries, that behave differently from stereotyped expectations of how a particular sex "should" behave. We'll look at some animals that change sex in chapter 7. Right now, we're going to talk about intersex animals, or those whose organs, hormones, or anatomy don't fall into a simple male or female category.

One of the most studied animals in North America is the white-tailed deer. (Pro tip: if an animal can be hunted or farmed, there are going to be a lot of studies on it, many of them funded by the US government.) White-tailed deer live in highly sex-segregated societies, in which the does live with their fawns and yearlings and the males stick to bucks-only bachelor groups of their own.

Studies in the 1960s, however, uncovered a third group of deer.

As they grow from yearlings into adults, all male deer go through a "velvet" stage, in which their growing horns are covered by soft fuzz. As they reach sexual maturity, the velvet is generally shed, revealing the bone antlers underneath. Some deer born with external male genitalia, though, never shed their velvet, and have bodies closer to those of female deer.

Known as velvet-horns, these intersex deer don't enter the pecking order of the rest of the deer society. In fact, they're soon driven out by the males. They skip the bachelor herds and the groups of mothers, and instead form their own troops of three to seven velvet-horns. Velvet-horns don't produce offspring, but live out healthy deer lives in their own velvet-horn societies.

All of the other mean deer used to laugh and call them names! They never let poor velvet-horns join in all the mean deer games!

Life as a velvet-horn sounds kind of awesome, actually. You hang out with your "found family" of like-minded deer, skip the work of birthing your own fawns, and avoid the deer-on-deer violence of the bachelor herds. Those antlers aren't just for show: males use them to fight one another. Competing for mates exhausts and wounds them, causing the males to lose up to one-quarter of their body weight. Velvet-horns are comparatively healthier, with what one researcher called (kind of cheekily, I think) "excellent body fat deposits."

This doesn't mean they're not interested in helping out. Since the velvet-horns don't mate, they don't produce their own offspring, but if they come across an orphaned fawn, they will incorporate them into their group to rear. A similar phenomenon happens among other species of deer, too: some mule deer are called "cactus bucks," owing to the pronged shapes on their small antlers. Behaviorally, they're identical to the velvet-horns: they have male genitalia but the body shapes of does, and stick to their own smaller cactus buck groups. Between 5 and 10 percent of the antlered fawns across studied deer species will not shed their velvet during their yearling months, and will instead grow into velvet-horns or cactus bucks. Similarly, nonreproductive intersex animals occur not just in white-tail deer and mule deer, but in red-tailed deer, swamp deer, sika, roe deer, fallow deer, and moose.

There is another sort of intersexuality in both the white-tail and mule deer. Though most females do not grow antlers, between 1 and 2 percent do. Some of those grow antlers with velvet, and some have shiny polished antlers, like fully mature males. Despite their male visual coding, these deer have fully functional female reproductive systems. They will mate with males and produce offspring, just like most female deer do. They just happen to have "male" antlers while they're doing so. In elk, some males don't grow antlers, giving them the appearance of females. Like the velvet-horn deer, they are in better physical condition than "normal" antlered males, but these elk *do* reproduce with females, and produce more offspring than their more traditional-looking male peers.

Reading a high school biology textbook, you might assume that animals have sex to make offspring, and that's it. But deer do plenty more that questions any easy assumptions about what gets to count as "natural sexual behavior" in the animal world.

For one, they'll masturbate. Males rub their penises against their own bellies, or stroke their antlers against clumps of vegetation to ejaculation. They also have homosexual sex: males will mount other males, and females will mount one another when in heat. Of the variety of sexual behaviors they undertake, these above are important to note because they are nonprocreative; that is, they don't lead to reproduction and offspring. The version of biology we all learn is that "survival of the fittest" causes animals to want to procreate at all

costs, but that's simply not true. They have a variety of sexual experiences and sexual motives—just like us. They have a variety of expressions of their sexual identities, too—also just like us.

This situation is not unique to deer, not in the least. Various dolphin and

Our antlers are sensitive, and rubbing them is very, um, sensual! Make sure you mention this next time you go over to your uncle's house with all those tough-guy antlers mounted on the wall.

whale species have intersex individuals that have genitalia of both sexes, including striped dolphins, bowhead whales, fin whales, and beluga. Males of many bird species undergo what's called "delayed plumage maturation," in which some young males grow female feathers for their first years. By "passing" as female, they avoid any aggression from males—and can be courted by them. Some garter snake males will give off female pheromones (signaling chemicals) so that other males will come to them and try to mate—to prevent them from mating with females or, according to an interesting new theory, perhaps to warm up their cold-blooded bodies with a big group snuggle! Playing with sexual expression can have fitness benefits, which helps explain why flexibility in sexual identities might have evolved.

Like in the case of the velvet-horn deer, there are many animals that do not ever reproduce. In some species, such as giraffes and right whales, estimates are that more than half of the population doesn't ever produce offspring. The proportion climbs much higher, to over 80 percent, for northern elephant seals and naked mole rats. In whiptail lizards, asexual females can produce fertile eggs without any sexual partner ever needing to be involved. They form social relationships with other females, courting them and pair bonding, only they don't have sex. Asexuality is just as much a part of the animal kingdom as other sexualities. Heterosexual procreation is not the norm in many species.

It is impossible to get inside another being's mind, whether human or non-human. But that doesn't mean that we cannot or should not consider what an animal is thinking or feeling. Though I don't have proof that an animal is feeling hunger, it's a logical enough assumption that they feel it. Animal hunger or animal pain doesn't have to be identical to human hunger or human pain for me to act with kindness and compassion, assuming they feel both. It just has to be similar enough. Likewise, an animal's experience of their own sex doesn't have to be identical to a human's for me to consider it and make reasonable assumptions about it. Doing so doesn't *equate* them with humans. It's just asking that we treat them with *equal consideration*.

The bar is very low on this front. The internal lives of animals are largely disregarded by science and agriculture, permitting us to abuse them with painful invasive testing or to submit them to horrific conditions in factory farms. When we see them as cogs of evolution, machines driven to propagate their genes and little more, then we can more easily feel permitted to exploit animals for our own ends without feeling guilt or hesitation. To return to the question that started the chapter (whether there are trans animals), the "other minds" problem keeps us from knowing for sure what an animal's experience is of their own sexuality and gender expression, just like we can't *know* they feel thirst or grief. Are there nonvelvet deer who perceive of themselves as velvet-horns, or vice versa? We can't really know. But are there animals who complicate any easy conceptions of male and female, and what those sexes "ought" to look like? Given the astonishing range in how sex is expressed in the animal kingdom, the answer is most certainly yes.

Q&A

BEANS VELOCCI

(EDITED FOR LENGTH AND CLARITY)

NAME: **BEANS VELOCCI**
PRONOUNS: **THEY/THEM**
TWITTER: **@BEANSVELOCCI**
JOB: **SCIENCE HISTORIAN**

ELIOT: I understand you're teaching a queer science course!

BEANS: I am, for the first time. It's a seminar that was capped at twelve students originally, but over fifty people applied and twenty-eight showed up for the first day. I think it's so indicative of an interest in the topic and also the need for it. Many STEM students are saying they haven't been getting this kind of content, that as queer people the things they're learning in biology class feel wrong.

ELIOT: How did you come to study the history of sexuality?

BEANS: I took a History of Gender and Sexuality course and had a light-bulb moment: "Oh, sex and gender are made-up things, and I don't have to do them! There's not something wrong with me, it's just a whole lot of nonsense used by the state, and science, to consolidate their power." I was just starting to come to my trans identity, and it was mind-blowing. Science and Technology Studies has a whole set of methods for thinking about classification and categories, and History of Sexuality is really interested in the formation of queer identities, but those fields largely aren't talking to each other. I figured: "Okay, someone needs to bring these two things together, and I guess that person is going to be me!"

Historians often say that sex science started in the 1870s to 1890s, but that's only if you're looking at humans. A lot of the early sex science was in animals—comparative zoology or agricultural sciences. They were grappling with a lot of the same questions of "what is sex, how does it work." When you look at these animal studies, it's clear that the way that scientists have defined sex over the past two centuries is wildly different depending on what they're trying to use it for.

ELIOT: Is there anything you'd like to change about your field?

BEANS: I'm interested in rethinking how people think about trans as a category. The way that a lot of trans history has unfolded in the past decade or so has been about looking for trans people in the past, which is important. But there's a way that you can do trans history that interrogates the sex binary, so instead of looking for exceptional expressions of sex and gender, we concentrate more on what's considered normal and why we think of it that way. I think of trans much more as a political tool than a classification tool, because I'm into picking apart classifications in general, and so I don't think there's an inherent way to classify people's gender at all. That said, I still identify as trans because I like to make myself legible as part of a shared experience, as part of a community, and to articulate a sense of politics.

ELIOT: Is "trans" a useful term to use for animals? Or even "gender"?

BEANS: I hesitate to ever say something like "seahorses are trans," or snails or whatever the case may be, because it doesn't sit well with me because of my own reluctance to classify. But I can also see the political utility. Like, speaking of seahorses, I know that among some trans dads who give birth, it's a bit of an identity, like they'll call themselves "seahorse dads." I think there's a source of comfort and legitimacy to be found there, even as I'm interested in asking why we turn to "nature" when making political and ethical claims.

I tell my dog all the time he's lucky that he doesn't have to have a gender because he's a dog. In human society, gender is not just about sex. Gender is made. It's about race, it's about class, it's about all these other things that are not present in the societies of nonhumans.

ELIOT: If you're willing to talk about how you identify, how has it worked in your career?

BEANS: I identify as trans, and nonbinary specifically, but I'm pretty "meh" about most other labels. I call myself queer, because it's one of the few ways to not have to name a gender identity in relation to someone else's when articulating a sexual identity. That's the level of precision that I'm most comfortable with. I feel like I'm able to critique categories from that perspective because I've already had to do a lot of work personally, so it's easier for me to say "okay, how are these categories being imposed, and how are they a bunch of made-up nonsense?" I do get misgendered at work all the time. Not usually in queer spaces or feminist spaces, but if I suddenly wander into the regular history world, I know people are going to call me the wrong thing, or not take my work seriously because I'm trans and therefore seen as "less objective." Then I ask them how their experience of gender makes them more objective about it, and usually they don't have an answer.

WANT TO LEARN MORE?

Beans is the author of "The Battle over Trans Rights Is about Power, Not Science," in the *Washington Post* (2018).

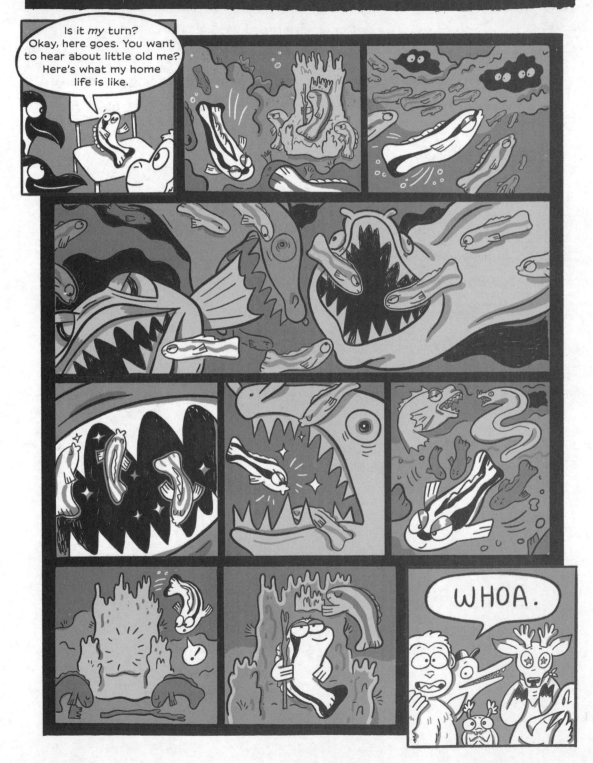

WRASSE FISH

DO ANIMALS CHANGE SEX?

STORY TIME

A tribe of warrior women lives under the sea. Every day they leave their palace of bone to venture into the cold depths, risking their lives to approach the forbidding caves of giant monsters.

The titans emerge. They are leviathans many thousands of times the women's size, opening their mouths to reveal razor-sharp fangs.

The women do not flee; instead they dance.

The beasts are transfixed. If the women are successful in their dancing, the monsters lower their heads, signaling that the ritual is complete. One by one, the women approach and groom them, passing along their bodies and even into their mouths, killing and consuming the parasites that live there.

The women return home, their bellies full. Now they must stand guard, hiding and watching the cold and salty depths. There are competitor tribes nearby, who could mount a challenge at any time.

The tribe has only one male. He spent the day patrolling his bone *kingdom, but now that the women are home, he returns. The male is the father of all their children, and he is merciless and dominating. He charges at the women, biting and bullying them into submission. The women put up with his aggression—for now. They are biding their time, waiting for a moment he lets down his guard . . . or gets eaten by the monsters in the depths.*

One day he goes off to fight an invader and doesn't return.

The women waste no time. The largest and most powerful comes forward to lead the tribe.

For an hour, and one hour only, peace reigns in their all-female society.

Then the leader starts changing. She bullies the others, nips and charges at them. She's as bad as the man was. Then, after just two hours, she is male! She's changed sex entirely.

There's no time to adjust, because the neighboring tribes have seen an opportunity. They attack the bone palace! Their warrior male is a hulking giant, and he bests the new leader in one-on-one combat. Does he kill him? No. Right in front of the tribe's eyes, their recently changed leader goes back to being a woman. She submits to their new outsider leader. She's watching and waiting, though—as soon as this invading man shows weakness, she'll launch an attack. And this time, she—or he, by then—won't fail.

It would make a good DC (or Marvel, I'm not taking sides!) superhero origin story. It's not the stuff of fantasy, though. It's fact. Here's our hero(ine):

Here she is doing some of her monster cleaning:

She's a bluestreak cleaner wrasse, a member of a family of reef fish that can be found just about anywhere there's coral to hide in. All female wrasses have the capacity to become male; only one will do so at a time, if she's at the top of the female hierarchy when the previous male dies. Within two hours, she'll have finished transitioning, and become the group's new male tyrant—though she'll change back if successfully challenged by a neighboring male.

This isn't unique to the bluestreak cleaner wrasse; sex reversal is common in fish. It's known as protandry if the fish goes from male to female, or protogyny as in our case of the cleaner wrasse, where females turn male. Though sex change occurs in lots of fish species, from eels to snooks, sea basses, tilefishes, porgies, wrasses, parrotfishes, and gobies, it is still not as common as "gonochoristic" fish, or those whose sex is determined at an early age and stays fixed for life.[*]

Another species of coral fish who change sex? Clown fish. They change in the opposite direction of wrasse—they're born male and turn female if conditions call for it. A handful of them will share an anemone to live in, but only the largest two ever enter the ultimate expression of their sex. One's male and

---

[*] Here's a fun fact to toss out at parties, if you go to nerd parties (which are obviously the best parties): "gonochoristic" is what's known as a *retronym*, or a word that's only necessary because a new opposing concept has been invented. Like how we didn't need the term "snail mail" until we invented "email." We just called it mail. "Heterosexual" is also a retronym; homosexual shows up first in the English language, and then everyone had to scramble to find a word to describe people who were attracted to people of the opposite sex. Linguistically speaking, gays came first. So did sex-changing animals. The straights and non-sex-changers came after.

one's female, and all the rest of the fish are smaller males. In their kingdom, there's a queen on top, a king under her, and then lots of presexual princes. If the queen dies, then the king turns into a queen, and one of the princes steps into the king role. Even though those "princes" might be just as old as the two in-charge fish, they're prevented from growing by "social domination," which is the scientific term for bullying.

Evolutionary biologists generally seek explanations for creatures' actions that are based on *fitness*, or how a behavior affects a) the creature's own survival and b) the chance of that creature's genes continuing in the next generation. Most often, those two things are in sync: if I survive to mating age, then I'm increasing the chance that my offspring will pass along my genes to future generations.

You know who else is a clown fish? Nemo. As in *Finding Nemo* Nemo. When (spoiler alert, but come on, who hasn't seen *Finding Nemo*?) his mother dies, Nemo's father, Marlin, should have become his mother. Come on, Pixar, that would have been amazing! I'd pay really good money to see that version of *Finding Nemo*.

Sometimes evolutionary fitness provides a perfectly reasonable explanation for why animals change sex. Some species of frogs and lizards, for example, change sex as needed within their local groups. If a freak accident takes out all the male frogs in a certain population, for example, rather than die out entirely, some of the females will change sex and begin to mate with the other females. That's a simple fitness-based explanation for sex changing—it keeps male-female ratios optimum so a species can avoid going extinct in any one area.

For the wrasse and the clown fish and the other sex-changing fish, though, this isn't a case of changing sex to prevent local extinction. Nothing has "gone wrong." Instead we're looking at sex change as an essential part of the social dynamics of the group; each member needs to have intimate awareness of the hierarchy for the right fish to change sex and the rest of the fish to accept it. It's an eternal power struggle that literally changes the bodies of those who participate.

There's a cost to changing sex for an animal. They don't need to pay medical bills, of course, but changing sex uses up energy in the form of calories, which can be risky when there's only so much food to go around. The general working scientific theory, then, is that an animal will change sex if a) the biological framework is there to make it possible (primates like humans, for example, don't have the capacity to change sex without medical intervention)* and b) the reproductive success of the animal becomes higher as the other sex.

If we think about it in sort of creepy economic terms, being male is less expensive than being female. Sperm are many thousandfold tinier than eggs, and so can be produced in greater quantity—which means that a sperm producer can potentially produce far more offspring than an egg producer. It's advantageous for your average wrasse female to become male, which is why they're all fighting to do it, and only the most aggressive will manage to succeed. Then that newly minted male gets to pass his genes to all the other females, and whatever body and behaviors led to him reaching that advantageous position get passed along, too. This is how sex change can evolve in the natural world.

In the case of the clown fish, the sole female does have the additional cost of producing eggs, but as the only egg producer in the group, she is the parent of every single member of the next generation, which is a benefit great enough to warrant the cost. She doesn't have it quite as made, evolutionarily speaking, as the sole male wrasse does, but getting her DNA into every young fish around is still a good gig—if she can hold on to it.

Flatworms are even more hard-core in their race to change sex. Rather than being "sequential hermaphrodites" like many fish (who go from male to female or

---

* Unlike gender, which is the socially constructed set of characteristics of one's sexual identity. See "What Queer Means," p. 25.

vice versa), flatworms are "simultaneous hermaphrodites." When two flatworms meet, each of them already has fully functional male and female organs. What happens is basically a sexual duel at high noon, only instead of pistols, the weapons of choice are penises. They draw them out, and it's a race to impale the other (and I do mean impale; they stab each other with those sharp things anywhere they can). It's thought that the winner's penis inserts allohormones that change the sexual behavior of the flatworm who's been stabbed. The flatworm who was slower on the draw begins the comparatively costly act of gestating offspring. The quicker flatworm goes about their day, carefree, while the now-female flatworm has a few hundred thousand eggs to raise.

Humans have plenty of sexual diversity in our identities and orientations, but sea creatures have us beat, hands (or should I say fins?) down. Like a lot of hermaphroditic aquatic creatures, flatworms also have the capacity to self-inseminate* if necessary. Other fish are parthenogenetic, which means they are all female, but require the sperm *from another species* to activate their own reproductive processes. That's really a lot to get your mind around; they pick up a guy who's not even their own species, have sex with him to begin the fertilization process, and then don't use his sperm at all, fertilizing their eggs themselves, with the sperm that's already in *their* body. I mean, what?!

As we've seen, the rainbow diversity of fishes goes way beyond coloration and into the ways they have sex. It goes even further than that, though, and into gender expression. Consider the parrotfish. Some parrotfish are born male, and some are born female. Simple enough so far. It all gets more complicated, however, when you consider that there are young males who don't have their full color, and matured males who are in full color, and the two gender expressions have totally different sexual tactics.

You should see the fish *pride flag!* Takes hours just to color it in.

---

* While animals are still commonly called "hermaphroditic" in scientific literature, the more accepted term when referring to humans is "intersex."

(Remember, too, the Nemo clown fish, where some males are "princes," with a much different gender expression than the more dominant "king.") Then we have to factor in that *all* female parrotfishes will eventually become male if they survive long enough. A scientific survey of the sex and gender identity of parrotfish turned up 45 percent females-at-birth who have not yet begun their male transformation, 27 percent males who were born females, 14 percent males-at-birth who have not yet gotten their mature colors and begun to mate, and 13 percent males-at-birth who had changed color and were enjoying their full parrotfish coloration and the more aggressive sexual techniques that come along with it.

Here's where the variety of sexual expression gets mind-blowing. Even when genetically identical, groups of parrotfish have many different *cultures* around sexual expression. In the waters near Jamaica, large groups of early-phase parrotfish will swarm and mate together, with the full-color late-phase males trying to break it all up. There, parrotfish have a "haremic" culture where one late-phase male keeps a pod of females for his exclusive mating. Some of the remaining fish live nonbreeding, asexual lives, not seeming to mind at

all that they've skipped over all that reproduction hullabaloo. In Puerto Rico and the Virgin Islands, parrotfish congregate in what are known as "leks," a specialized sort of arena in which both male genders work together to create the perfect conditions to attract females. They collaborate to arrange everything just right, adjusting shells and rocks to get the colors and patterns of the environment perfect. The equivalent of putting mood music on in the background.

Because of their variety of sexual expression, we can say that fish have up to five genders, depending on the species. The idea of a nonhuman animal having different gender expressions is already a big enough deal. But there's also the astonishing fact that parrotfish have *different cultures depending on where they live.* Culture is the regional variation of behaviors within a species, and for a while, it was thought that only humans had it. Then scientists grudgingly agreed to expand that concept to our closest relatives, the great apes. One group of chimpanzees might use leaves as bowls to scoop water out of the hollows of trees, for example, while another group a few hundred miles away might never do that—but they have a hand gesture that the first group doesn't use, and so on.

There's a whole lot more to fish than most of us allow. Even those who really love land animals can turn a cold heart to fish. They don't emote using the same methods that mammals do, but just because they don't bare their teeth or wag their tails doesn't mean that they don't have sentience and feelings. It's easy to assume there's nothing going on upstairs with fish, but there's clearly quite a bit to a fish's internal life. Young fish are learning how their particular society works, not just behaving on instinct. And that means genetically identical fish might behave differently around the Virgin Islands than around Puerto Rico, because they're learning from their parents and the other fish around them.

It's not just fish. Frogs and lizards will change sex, and having male and female genitalia is the standard way of life for the majority of plants. One of my favorite animal hermaphrodites, though, has to be the sea snail. They're all born male, and once two males meet-cute and fall in love, one of them simply changes sex. Much later, after she's finished with her first partner, that now-female snail might meet a different male and stay female. What makes this example endearing to me is that, in laboratory studies, some males kept choosing other males, even though they'd then have to wait a few days for their partner to change sex, while other males always went for females. The snails had preferences. Snails!

If we tend not to give enough thought to the internal lives of fish, we definitely don't do so for sea snails. And yet here they are making choices as individuals, and some of them show what we could consider a homosexual orientation, i.e., choosing exclusively partners of their own sex. As the scientists behind the aforementioned snail studies put it, this illustrates "the importance of active choice in the behavior of species that are generally considered to possess little agency over their reproductive fitness." In other words, snails are gonna snail, and they're stubborn about it.*

The animal world has a lot to teach us about how commonplace changing sex is. It also shows that it's normal to have an existence that is outside of male and female, and to be flexible in partner preference—that there is widespread diversity in how nonhumans answer the question of which sex they "should" be attracted to. They have partners whose pronouns (if they used them) might change multiple times over their lifetimes, and it's no big deal. An animal can prefer subordinate males or dominant females, they can like females that used to be male, males that used to be female, or they can skip over sex and repro-duction entirely and live asexual lives. It's all fine.**

---

* Another thing that made me laugh about this particular snail study was that it takes a few days for snails to change sex, so the researchers were in a quandary—how would they determine the sex of a snail that was in the middle of transitioning? They developed their own methodology to figure out how to report the sex of each snail they examined. They settled on this: "Snails were determined to be male if their penis was longer than either of their tentacles." Just some old-school penis-tentacle comparison. In all seriousness, I wish scientists would let themselves log transitioning animals not as male or female at all but something else—but the scientific need to assign male or female appears to be deeply ingrained.

** This discussion can touch on some concepts and ideas that are similar to concepts in the sex lives of humans, but it's one case where the parallels only go so far. Humans can change gender expression without surgery, but we generally can't change sex that way, except for the case of some rare medical conditions which unexpectedly alter development during puberty. Sex reassignment surgery in humans is a large undertaking, whose financial costs and medical risks are significant. It takes a lot of planning and courage on the part of whoever's going through it. It's also the result of a choice resulting from a mismatch between someone's sex and gender identity. That's quite different from the socially caused changing of sex in animals, in which animals change sex spontaneously based on the needs of the group, or based on their particular position in a dominance hierarchy. There is one irrefutable takeaway, though: changing sex occurs throughout the animal world.

JESSIE BUSHELL

Q&A

MAX LAMBERT
(EDITED FOR LENGTH AND CLARITY)

NAME: **MAX LAMBERT**
PRONOUNS: **HE/HIM**
TWITTER: **@MAXRLAMBERT**
JOB: **CONSERVATION BIOLOGIST**

ELIOT: What's been your journey as a scientist and a researcher?

MAX: I had a really good public high school teacher who managed to string together a bunch of grants to teach an ecology class. He brought students out into the field to track mountain lions, study insects and water pollution. I was like, "Oh, this is a thing that people actually do. It's not just David Attenborough on TV."

ELIOT: You don't have to have a fancy English accent to do it!

MAX: Right. So I went to college to do a degree in wildlife biology. Before that time, I had viewed science as a finished thing, like science is *done*. But science is something we will never finish; it's always progressing and changing as our worldview changes. I got really interested in toxicology, and was really focused on all the various chemical pollutants in our food and water and air. My master's and PhD work was centered on a group of chemical pollutants that have been called estrogen mimics. That's what got me into understanding sex and animals in a very different way, because the same words for animals suffering from pollutants were used to attack the queer community and even just to attack women. The idea that switching sexes is bad is filled with a very toxic transphobic, homophobic, sexist rhetoric about what it means being female, and implies that being female is worse than being male or male-like. The more data I collected in the wild populations, the more that narrative just didn't make sense. I found frogs switching sex all over the place, males turning to females and females turning to males—in the most natural, pristine places, without any pollutants in them. It took me, you know, an hour and a half to hike to that pond.

ELIOT: And there was no glowing green barrel of toxic waste anywhere nearby.

MAX: Exactly, exactly. Switching sex wasn't negative or positive, it was just part of the natural state of that population. Biologists told ourselves for so long that it must be unnatural. My research led to a good question: Why do queer things exist? The simple answer is that animal bisexuality is not costly. It was so biologically simple. We're publishing another paper now on sex reversal. Again, very, very natural. It seems like it is a thing that just happens.

ELIOT: Have there been barriers to publishing on sex reversal or same-sex sexual behavior?

MAX: Absolutely. A paper I published in 2019 on sex reversal being very common in frogs . . . I think I submitted it to nine or ten different journals. We got very positive reviews back, but after every indication it was going to be published, they just went, "nah." The journal is basically saying, "We don't want to rock the boat."

ELIOT: If you were talking to a high school biology class that has learned only from their textbook, what would you tell them?

MAX: It's a book that's in progress, and always will be. We will always be changing our view of the world and updating it as we learn more and more. And that's a scary thing, because you'll never have something you're very settled with. The idea that anything has discrete categories, whether it's sex or something else, is rarely true. And so when someone says "it's this or that, A or B, one or two," there's always some other option out there. Be open to that, because even male and female itself is less clear-cut than you may have thought growing up.

ELIOT: If you're willing to discuss your various identifications, how have they influenced your career, if at all?

MAX: I am a cisgender, heterosexual white male. I don't have an identity that had allowed me to really sympathize with marginalized communities in any meaningful way. And it was having queer female colleagues say "yeah, I've wanted to study what you're studying too. But everyone else kept saying how feminization was bad. And I didn't wanna be part of that, because that was just like a toxic thing for me to read about every day."

ELIOT: It sounds like it was a burden that was easier for you to carry, since you weren't directly implicated by the language.

MAX: We reinforce a lot of marginalized social inequalities, systemic racism, in the way we do science in urban areas. That's extraordinarily problematic. Science is done by scientists. And if you have a very narrow culture of who's doing science, you're going to end up with a very narrow view of how life actually works on this planet. The benefit of diversity in sciences is that you get all these various perspectives and experiences that allow you to challenge the idea that same-sex behavior is an unnatural state.

WANT TO LEARN MORE?

Max is the author (with Julia D. Monk, Erin Giglio, Ambika Kamath, and Caitlin E. McDonough) of "An Alternative Hypothesis for the Evolution of Same-Sex Sexual Behaviour in Animals" in *Nature Ecology & Evolution* (2019), in which the authors "hypothesize an ancestral condition of indiscriminate sexual behaviours directed towards all sexes."

Max is also the author (with Melina Packer) of "How Gendered Language Leads Scientists Astray," in the *Washington Post*, 2019.

CHAPTER EIGHT: ALBATROSS

ALBATROSS

DOES SEXUALITY REQUIRE SEX?

Let's say you have an Aunt Therese. Therese gives the best birthday presents. She's also lived with the same woman for decades, Aunt Carol. They've both been strong presences in your life, so much so that you had to ask just a couple of years ago which one was your mom's sister. (It was Carol. Or Therese. Now you can't remember all over again. Go check with your mom and come back.)

Carol and Therese met when they were twenty. They decorate their gardening overalls with puffy paint. They bought and rebuilt a house together. They have matching reindeer sweaters that they wear when they come over at the holidays, the kind where Rudolph's red nose lights up. One prepares a cup of coffee before the other says out loud that she'd like one. They have posters of Megan Rapinoe and Tegan and Sara. They adopted children, raised them, and now those kids are off at college and raising children of their own. Therese and Carol have already bought adjoining plots at the local cemetery. They're in it for life, through thick and thin, never to part.

When that one middle school friend was confused about why Carol and Therese lived in the same house, you said simply, "They're lesbians. Like, life partners," and your friend said, "Okay, cool," and that was the end of that.

You never asked them about their sex life. Frankly, you always figured it was their business. Or maybe you really never gave it a single thought, because reindeer sweaters. Or maybe you never asked because then they'd feel like they were allowed to ask about *your* sex life, and no one wanted that to happen.

What if you find out one day that Carol and Therese don't have sex? Like, you're watching some movie that has a sex scene, and Carol laughs and says, "Maybe we should have tried that out after all, Therese?"

What if they've *never* had sex?

Are they still lesbians?

Most of us are probably saying yes at this point. They've spent their lives together, they have those posters of Megan Rapinoe and Tegan and Sara.

What if Carol technically lied about never being with anyone else—she had sex with a boy while she was in high school. She hated it, and decided that she was just not interested in having sex again. But she is so into Therese. Cuddles with Therese, shares her home and life with Therese, maybe kisses Therese, but for whatever reason doesn't like to have sex, and so Carol and Therese don't. Technically, Carol has had sex with one male and zero females. So what now?

On the human side of things, this isn't really much of a gray zone. Therese and Carol are lesbians if they say they're lesbians. They get to self-identify how they like, and people should follow their wishes on that front. They're two romantically attached women spending their lives together, and if they self-describe as lesbians, then no one has any business putting their nose in there and telling them otherwise.

(By the way, there are very many unions—gay, straight, and otherwise—in which the partners don't have sex. Sometimes the relationship started sexual, and then it tapered off. Or the partners have sex outside the union. Or one or more parties in the relationship are ace, meaning that they don't experience sexual attraction. There have been many, many Thereses and Carols throughout history. There was a particular bloom in female-female households in New England in the late nineteenth and early twentieth century, enough that the term "Boston marriage" came to describe women cohabitating and spending their lives together, whether the union was sexual or not.)

It's a different story in the animal world. We can't ask animals to self-identify because they're unable to speak to us, and so science has approached their sex lives with a narrow lens. As far as science is concerned, sex is something that can be tabulated in a logbook, quantifiable and irrefutable. "Creature A had sex x times per cycle with Creature B," that sort of thing. When animals can be treated like machines, science is able to interpret their behavior. But when they're considered as beings with their own subjective experience of the world, then it becomes much harder to interpret their lives—and their sex lives in particular—with the sort of quantifiable clarity that "good science" prefers.

For a long time, the simple solution was to deny animals their subjectivity. To see them as robotic results of instincts, not beings with thoughts and feelings.

But there's a lot of middle territory that scientific studies haven't allowed for until recently, animal behaviors that don't fit into easy sex-based distinctions. In nesting birds particularly, it turns out there are a whole lot of Carols and Thereses.

One of the beauties of queerness is that it resists simple definitions and classifications. I'm not trying to claim here that female-female pairs of nesting birds are lesbians, just like it's not my business to label your aunts Carol and Therese. However. I'm not saying that those birds *aren't* lesbians, either.

Queerness doesn't require us to decide one way or the other.

We're about to examine pairs of female birds that elect to spend their entire lives as a couple, going to great lengths in nesting season to find each other so they can nest together again, raising offspring from eggs that have been fertilized by a male outside the union. These females court each other, but never mate. Their examples force us to evaluate how we think about animal sexuality. How much weight do we give to the sex act itself, compared to other qualities of romantic partnership, like attraction and commitment and—to use a term that would make any classically trained biologist pass out right on the spot—love?

How would you define love, anyway? Given how tricky a concept it is for humans to get a handle on, even when applied to our own species, would we be so stingy to keep from considering it as being even a possibility for other animals?

Let's take a look at an animal that we could think of as a model of love.

The Laysan albatross is one of the largest birds on earth, with a wingspan upward of six and a half feet. At their size, it's pretty hard for them to get airborne—go look up blooper reels of albatrosses trying to take off to see what I mean. But once they're in the air, albatrosses are gentle experts of air currents, able to go hours without a single flap of their wings. The jumbo jets of the animal world, they can travel enormous distances in one go, journeying for thousands of miles without landing. Though they nest on the Hawaiian Islands, Laysan albatrosses fly as far as California or Japan to feed. They're able to do so through what's known as "dynamic soaring," strategically altering their altitude to find currents going in the right direction for their use, and exerting very little energy in the process.

They're also unusually long-lived, only starting to breed once they're eight or nine years old, and living up to around sixty-five years. During this time they form lasting pair bonds, returning to raise chicks year after year with the same partner. Together they spend decades perfecting their parenting techniques. After a summer spent apart, each November they come together and reaffirm the relationship through an elaborate bonding ritual that looks a lot like a dance.

They touch bills and nod heads and do a sort of dab move with their head under one wing and the other wing pointed to the sky.

For nearly a third of the pairs, these partners are both female. They go through all the same courtship behaviors as male-female pairs and are equally devoted parents. The only difference is that one or both of the females slips away to mate with a male from outside the union, so her eggs can get fertilized. Male albatrosses, it seems, have no problem whatsoever with a little mating on the side of their own unions. He'd better not try to move in on the relationship, though: as researcher Lindsay Young observed, the female couples "behave just like male-female pairs . . . if a male comes up to one female in the pair, the second female gets really possessive."

Sometimes only one female gets inseminated, so there's just one chick to care for; in other cases both females are fertilized, so they have two young birds to look after, what's known as a "supernormal clutch." It's not easy having twice the brood. Double the offspring means plenty of extra work, as the chicks consume a lot of food, which makes their survival outcomes lower in these cases. It also can mean that a female who's already expended a lot of energy producing an egg will have to take a three-week shift incubating that egg rather than flying off to feed right away (in male-female pairs, it's the male who takes the first incubating shift, since he didn't have to produce an egg and has more gas in the tank).

Still, two females raising two eggs together have better outcomes than either female would have on her own. This has led some scientists to argue that these otherwise single parents are "making the best of a bad job" in response to a shortage of males. This is part of a long trend to explain away same-sex behavior in animals through negative explanations (see Introduction). Obviously these females would have preferred to be with a male, the scientists claim, but if they can't do that, then they'll settle for another female.

Sure, it's possible that these female albatrosses are indeed "making the best of a bad job." There is a strong drive to explain away female pairing in particular in scientific literature, reducing it to "females getting by" rather than considering it a chosen union. Remember Paul Vasey (chapter 5), who argues that "researchers have been blinded by the prevailing preoccupation to find adaptive explanations for every behavior" and that, in Japanese macaque monkeys, female-female sex can come about easily even with no shortage of available males. "By and large the females were more interested in other females—they're bisexual, not preferentially heterosexual." In other words, even without an evolutionary explanation, female-female choice is persistent and prevalent.

It's entirely possible that there is no easy "adaptive" evolutionary explanation for why 31 percent of Laysan albatross couples are female-female. Just like how we don't require evolutionary explanations for a lot of the life choices humans make: it's just what they choose.

If we want to go searching for adaptive explanations for female-female nesting in Laysan albatrosses, though, there are plenty to be found. One particularly intriguing theory is that female-female bonding might have evolved in nesting birds because it allows each sexually active male to fertilize more females. While each female produces only one egg each season, one male can produce millions of sperm. So a population that evolves to have more females, with a third of those females bonding with each other in lifelong unions, actually can raise more total chicks than a population in which every partnership is male-female.

Imagine an extreme case:

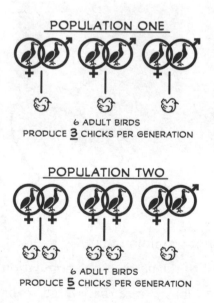

POPULATION ONE

6 ADULT BIRDS
PRODUCE **3** CHICKS PER GENERATION

POPULATION TWO

6 ADULT BIRDS
PRODUCE **5** CHICKS PER GENERATION

This is a thought exercise, and of course nothing in the wild comes out exactly according to the math. Rats or sharks will eat albatross chicks that aren't well attended, and that could be why one study shows slightly lower survivorship for chicks raised in supernormal clutches with overworked female-female parents. Not all female clutches, furthermore, are "supernormal"—they might have just one egg to raise. However, even if lower survivorship makes the difference here less dramatic, you can still see how this makes for a compelling adaptive explanation as to why female pair bonding has evolved in nesting birds. "Lesbian" bonding leads to more total chicks! This led historian and ornithologist Jared Diamond to dryly declare that "further study of homosexually paired female birds may help clarify what, if anything, males are good for—in an evolutionary sense, of course."

Laysan albatrosses are not outliers, not by a long shot. They just happen to be one of the few animal populations that's been studied specifically for same-sex pairings. Most birds are like the penguins: sexually monomorphic, meaning that males and females are the same size, without external genitalia. So in the case of a bird like an albatross or a penguin, most observers would have no idea whether they were seeing a male or female, which means there

have been centuries of unchecked assumptions in the scientific literature about nests always being tended by heterosexual pairs. Open your biology textbook, and you're likely to find that assumption on full display.

Some scientists have devoted themselves to making up for lost time on that front, using modern techniques to determine the sex of nesting birds, and finding out how prevalent female-female nesting is across all bird species. Researcher Lindsay Young notes that female-female nesting is found in "not just albatrosses,

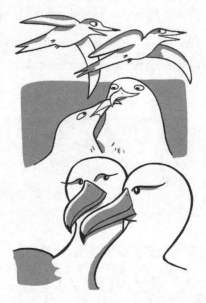

but other seabirds as well. This may be a lot more common than we realized, so the race is on to find out." About 12 percent of the nests in one population of roseate terns (a type of adorable small shorebird) were discovered to be female-female. Similar percentages of female-female nesting are found in gulls and jackdaws. In these species, females will make a joint nest, a large structure with separate spots for each bird's eggs. In Canada geese and mute swans, the female pairs will construct separate but adjacent nests.

Male bird couples don't have the possibility of laying eggs of their own, but that doesn't stop them from coming together, either. Male mute swans may bond for life just like female pairs do, even though their nests are empty. Same for black-crowned night herons and great cormorants. There is also a tendency across bird species for birds with too many eggs to care for to "give" them to couples with fewer or no eggs in their own nests. This has classically been called "parasitism," as observers—in their search for evolutionarily selfish reasons for behaviors—have assumed it to be trickery. What looks like manipulation through one observer's eyes, though, looks like donation and adoption through another's.

Since Darwin's time, great strides have been made into studying the persistence of altruism within animals. On the surface, altruism—one animal working to help another unrelated individual—shouldn't exist in the "survival of the fittest" conception of evolution. And yet it does. Social insects, like bees and ants, are an extreme example: they will sacrifice their lives to protect the community. They are so highly related, though, that evolutionary biologists can argue that their self-sacrifice is also selfish; when every member of the hive is your genetic sister, dying to save them is also making sure your own genes survive to get passed along.

Altruism springs up, however, in groups where the animals aren't closely related. Vervet monkeys will make alarm calls to warn other monkeys of danger, even if it means attracting a predator to themselves. Vampire bats will regurgitate blood to feed other bats who didn't manage to feed that night, so they don't starve (so sweet, puking up blood for one another!). And, across bird species, "helper" birds will help guard a nesting pair's nest—or take over ownership

of eggs if the host pair has too many to care for. Maybe selfishness isn't the only rule of the day.

Every time I ask swans or herons whether their egg swapping to benefit male-male nesting pairs should be considered parasitism or adoption, they refuse to tell me the answer. Rude! Without any input from the birds themselves, the question remains unresolved. If we allow for the possibility that animals have an emotional experience of the world and aren't just mechanical products of genetic drives, it becomes clear that perhaps these same-sex animal couples simply derive pleasure from raising young, just like human parents of adopted children do. Maybe the emotional instinct to care for young is present in the birds' minds, even when those baby birds aren't biologically their own. That instinct had a very good reason for evolving, even if it winds up getting applied to a nestling that doesn't share its parents' genetics. It's not an unreasonable explanation at all.

The adoption of young by same-sex pairs isn't limited to birds. Pairs of male cheetahs will parent lost cubs, and female pairs of northern elephant seals adopt orphaned pups. This has led some theorists to argue that by having a small subset of homosexual pairs as the natural state of their communities, animal populations have a built-in safety net of willing childless parents ready to take over should a young creature's birth parents meet an untimely end.

In the bird examples above, same-sex parenting begins with courtship and elaborate rituals of partner choice, just like it does for heterosexual pairs. If we consider same-sex parents that don't also exhibit courtship or sexual behavior, the numbers found in nature skyrocket. As Bruce Bagemihl observes in *Biological Exuberance*, "sometimes two female animals who already have offspring join forces, bonding together and raising their young as a same-sex family unit (among mammals, female coparents may even suckle each other's young): this occurs in Grizzly Bears, Red Foxes, Warthogs, Dwarf Cavies, Lesser Scaup Ducks, and Sage Grouse." As he goes on to point out, these are all species in which the norm is single parenting; parenting in a same-sex household isn't duplicating what happens in heterosexual households—in these species there is *no* heterosexual parenting!

In still other species, such as squirrel monkeys and greater rheas, a breeding animal will join with a nonbreeding animal of the same sex, and the two will raise the offspring together. Often this comes about because the breeding animal has been widowed; with no pressure to get fertilized, the parent might turn to a partner of the same sex.

The fiercest parenting award has to go to black swans, in which male pairs use their combined strength to nab the best territory away from hetero pairs. These ferocious males will invite a female in, only to chase her away once she's laid her fertilized egg. They then raise the chick on their own. (Read more about swans in chapter 10.)

Sexuality involves a lot more than sex. That goes for humans, and it goes for animals. There are plenty of human couples of all sorts who have lots of sex. There are also plenty of homosexual couples who never have sex, plenty of bisexual couples who never have sex, and plenty of heterosexual couples who never have sex. Just like being a virgin doesn't stop a straight person from being straight, actual sex isn't a prerequisite for having a sexuality. These examples of animals who form same-sex partnerships, who choose as the most important other creature in their life a member of the same sex, show what great diversity there is to animal sexuality and animal life choices.

Just like human sexuality and gender identification, just like all of our human couplings of Thereses and Carols, and Terrences and Curts, and Thereses and Curts, and Carols and Terrences, and Terrences and Carols and Thereses, and Carols all alone, animal sexuality resists simplification. It certainly doesn't march neatly onto an ark in boy-girl pairs.

CHAPTER NINE: BULLS

BULLS

WHAT COULD BE MANLIER THAN
SEX BETWEEN A COUPLE OF MALES?

Simon Amor spends his work life extracting semen from bulls. It's risky business, getting a dangerous two-thousand-pound animal sexually excited and then leaping in there at the last moment to steal his semen. Once he's gotten the bull worked up, Amor says, "We use what we call an 'artificial vagina,' which has a vial attached, and place the bull's penis inside. That's how we collect the semen."

He'll do this twenty times a day and has been on the job for twenty years. Do the math, and that's many, many barrels of bull semen. Swimming pools' worth. And he's far from the only person doing this. The process is repeated across the world. As of the writing of this chapter, the US cattle herd numbers over 2,237,000 bulls—and the majority of their inseminating is done artificially, using techniques like Simon Amor's.

If the bull is excited enough, it's all over quickly. "Bulls don't need any foreplay at all," Amor explains. As long as they're in the mood, that is.

When each bull is ejaculated two to three times a week, and two or three times each ejaculation day, they can start resisting. There are ways to get the bull feeling frisky—Amor can stroke the bull down the back of his leg, for example—but by and large he tries not to get the bulls *too* excited. "It's too much of a risk. The only thing you use to control a bull is a piece of rope and a nose ring. While the nose ring will slow him up a bit, he's going to go where he wants to go."

Why not just let cows and bulls hang out in a field and create the next generation the natural way? Because dairy and beef are big industries, and farmers make a lot more profit from cattle that grow quicker and produce more flesh and biofluids. Once semen is extracted from a prize bull, it can be sold to the highest bidder, packed in dry ice, and mailed anywhere in the world to impregnate cows. If a bull is known to produce especially profitable young, the price for his semen will go up and up. Some recent sales pamphlets for prize bull semen touted the output of Sanchez, who "makes them special—tall, dairy and strong with beautiful udders," or GW Atwood, "the hottest bull to hit the type market in years." In 2019 an Angus bull broke records by selling for $1.5 million—thanks to his eternal supply of that precious semen.

If buyers are waiting for an expensive batch of bull semen, they're not going to be happy if it's late to their heifers. But bulls aren't sex machines, and while they might not need much foreplay, they still need to be in the mood. Sometimes stroking the bull down the leg just won't cut it. The more reliable way to get him in the mood is to trot out another bovine for him to look at.

By and large, that pinup beefcake is a male. That's right, the cattle industry, that most red-blooded of American livelihoods, land of the cowboys

I like the sexy steers technique. A lot. Much better than "electroejaculation," which involves an electric probe and my rectum. Uh-uh.

and the Marlboro man, has been relying on same-sex attraction for years and years.

There are practical reasons for this. The mood-setting steer isn't going to be impregnated by accident, and if there's less chance of penetration there's less chance of STDs getting passed around the cattle population, which is a big problem in an industry that has so many animals pressed into close quarters. But those complications don't take away the fact that castrated males are the ace card in the sex lives of bulls.

Of course, as we've seen in most of the animals we've studied, bisexuality is really the rule of the day in the animal kingdom. It should be unsurprising by now to learn that bulls are aroused by other males. Males' tendency to mount other males, and females' tendency to mount other females, is so widespread that it attracts little notice from cattle breeders; it's just a common occurrence, part of being around cattle. In fact, females will mount other females so often that farmers will use that to identify when they're in heat. "Elsie's after Bertha again, looks like she's ready for another calf," that sort of thing.

It's possible to dismiss the bull/steer love connection by saying the situation they're in is artificial. In their natural environment, wouldn't bulls surely prefer a heifer to a steer?

Often not, it turns out. First off, if a bull has gotten used to steers, he'll begin to favor them entirely over female cows. The bulls Simon Amor extracts semen from will *never* be with a female in their lives, and could be said in that case to live exclusively homosexual lives, because of the human-created semen-milking system they find themselves trapped in.

But that bull has only ever had access to males. Take him out of that environment and he'll mate with females . . . right?

In general, yes. But oftentimes no.

Once they're in the pasture, male cattle will run a bit wild. Here's how one bovid scientist described it:

> *Male-male mounting can be so frequent in domestic bovids that it is considered to be a problem for the cattle industry. The "buller-steer syndrome" is characterized by the persistent following and repeated mounting of a steer (referred to as "buller") by one or a group of steers (known as "riders").*

It's enough of a persistent drive among males that it can all get out of hand. And the females are no different:

> *Cattle in mixed-sex herds will sometimes congregate into all-female subgroups when some or all females are in estrus. In these groups, females engage in the same courtship behaviours common to mating bulls, including genital licking, chin rubbing and mounting.*

What is going on here? Cattle have complicated brains, and many external markers of sex. They should have no trouble determining who they're mating with. There's the visual difference, with udders and horns and penises all clearly marking who's who, and cattle also use scent to distinguish individuals and determine their sex.

So cattle (and probably doodlebugs) know just fine whether they're pursuing a male or a female, yet they still engage in same-sex sex. Why? This frequent same-sex activity doesn't do much to enhance reproduction, right?

Stop talking about me like I'm not even here!!!

Sure, but it doesn't do much to hinder it, either— and that's the key. Homosexual activity in cattle doesn't have to have a reason to exist other than sexual gratification. In other words, they do it because it feels good—that much is unmistakable from their gusto around the activity. Cattle have evolved to arouse easily, for reasons that have everything to do with producing more offspring. That arousal finds outlet in both sexes; that doesn't mean that same-sex desire has to have evolved directly in cattle. It could just be a harmless by-product of evolution building a stronger and stronger sex drive in cattle in general.

It's not just cattle, either: the same tendency toward same-sex behavior in males and females is widespread in other bovids, like bison and sheep. That's an easier pill to swallow for some people than others. Often these observations were couched in judgmental language: a bison scientist who observes the "unnatural" bonds between mounting males, or a study discussing the "male homosexual vice" of sex between bulls. For the most part, though, cattle ranchers seem to have been very chill about their largely bisexual herds, even those ranchers who don't extend similar open-mindedness to bisexual humans.

Some domestic sheep take it even further. There are male bighorns with an exclusive preference for other males. As in, they will refuse female sheep, want nothing to do with female sheep, are here for only the male sheep. Nearly 8 percent of them fall into this category, according to one study, and another study conducted at the US Sheep Experimentation Center in Dubois, Idaho, found that over a three-year period the number varied anywhere between 15 and 30 percent. These males choose rams over ewes every time, but otherwise went through the same courtship steps—only ending in anal penetration rather than vaginal.

The existence of exclusively homosexual sheep gets farmers distinctly *unre*-laxed. Sheep make big money, and having a ram who doesn't want to perform with the ewes can be costly. In order to maximize overall production, farmers will have many more ewes than they have rams, and buying a good breeding ram costs them anywhere from $350 for a cheapie to $4,000 for a prime stud. If one of those rams doesn't live up to his "duties," then it's a loss for the farmer. As one government investigator put it, "No matter how many bullets are in the clip, nothing happens until firing commences." A ram who isn't interested in females is termed a "dud stud."

Some nerve.

He's certainly not a dud to the males, it turns out! One of the foremost sheep researchers has been observing the animals in the Rockies for decades, his research beginning during the 1960s, when homosexuality was widely reviled. Because he didn't want to think of his study animals as engaging in same-sex behaviors, he tried to explain it away. "I still cringe at the memory of seeing old D-ram mount S-ram repeatedly," he reports. "To conceive of those magnificent beasts as 'queers.' Oh God!" He went through great labors to frame the same-sex behavior within sheep not as sex at all, but as an elaborate means of establishing a hierarchy. Ultimately, even if it had a secondary goal of establishing a sheep hierarchy, he couldn't deny the fact that he was witnessing sheep of the same sex experience sexual pleasure together. A lot. They might also be establishing a power dynamic, sure, but they were unmistakably having sex. "Eventually I . . . admitted that the rams lived in essentially a homosexual society."

In the wild, sheep live in separate male and female herds, engaging in homosexual sex except during the rutting season, when males and females come together for reproduction only; like with deer, the males do not bond with particular females or participate in rearing their offspring.

Sheep courting one another, whether the combination is heterosexual or homosexual, have all sorts of sexy moves. They'll twist their head and flick their tongue with a "come hither" look. They'll take a lick of each other's urine. They'll kick their foreleg into each other's crotch . . . which I guess must feel good? The process is the same, whether it's two ewes or two rams or hetero courtship.

Sometimes three to ten sheep of the same sex will get together and have what scientists have called a "huddle." It's not like a football huddle, or at least not like most football huddles. I won't go into details, but there's a whole lot more rubbing and mounting. Same-sex courtship is such a big thing in bighorn sheep culture that some females will mimic males, taking on their "typical male" behaviors, or males will similarly mimic females, just in order to join the action.

This public outing of the habits of cows and sheep occurred in the late 1980s and early 1990s, which also happened to be a time when human homosexuality was an especially scandalous topic in the news. The AIDS crisis had hit the queer community hard, and in response the conservative establishment had entrenched against the "gay cancer" and the "promiscuity" that had led to a general decline of "family values." Under the guise of protecting the "traditional family," Vice President Dan Quayle publicly bemoaned the prospect of gays being parents. The government shelved an $18 million survey of teen sex health and canceled a million-dollar study into the diversity of adult sexual behavior, which had been established to help stem the burgeoning AIDS epidemic.

It amounted to a government moratorium on any funding for studies of queerness, across all bureaus and agencies—with one notable exception: the Department of Agriculture. They were still trying to work out a solution to the "dud-stud phenomenon" in order to help America's farmers. Not only was animal homosexuality on the docket for government study, it was the *only* form of queer sexuality the United States was willing to consider. Humans? No thank you.

That study aimed to determine whether there was a hormonal basis to same-sex desire in stud rams, but came out with no conclusions—except that, given a choice of male or female sex partners, a good proportion of rams would choose males, time and again. Farmers were warned "not to be blinded by large testicles" when choosing a ram to purchase. That is, a ram might look healthy and virile and have plenty of sperm to spare, but if he's not into female sheep, the farmer would be out their investment, up to $4,000.

Rams and bulls and bison aren't just any old animal in the culture of the United States, right? They're also the ultimate symbols of our rugged frontier version of masculinity. Think of our sports teams, the LA Rams, the Chicago Bulls. The Dodge Ram and Chevrolet Bison trucks. The rodeo, our American-ized version of the bullfighting traditions of Europe that prizes the aggressive virility of the bull and matador above all else.

Rams and bulls and bison are also some of the few animals that can be said to have individuals that are exclusively gay or lesbian, not just bisexual.

No one knows what the sheep's and cattle's experience of all this is, of course, and it's too bad we can't ask them for their take. Certainly the research and public opinion around them has, as always, as much to say about human attitudes as it does about the animals' own sexuality. But there's a particular irony to this case, where the "manliest" of animals are the ones closest to our own spectrum of sexualities, down to the percentage of the population that swears off heterosexual interaction entirely.

Q&A

LOGAN WEYAND

(EDITED FOR LENGTH AND CLARITY)

NAME: **LOGAN WEYAND**
PRONOUNS: **HE/HIS**
WEBSITE: **LOGAN'S RESEARCH GROUP ON MAMMALIAN ECOLOGY AND
CONSERVATION: RACHLOWLAB.WEEBLY.COM/PEOPLE.HTML**
JOB: **VETERINARIAN AND WILDLIFE ECOLOGY PHD STUDENT**

ELIOT: You've spent a lot of time with wild bighorn sheep, studying their susceptibility to disease. At one point in this book I quote Valerius Geist, a famous sheep researcher who eventually said he had to confess that young male sheep live in what's basically a homosexual society. Have you witnessed same-sex sexual behavior in sheep?

LOGAN: I'm thinking he's referring to same-sex mounting, and I've definitely seen that. Between two male sheep, or between lambs. I'll be careful here and say that I don't have their perspective on why they're doing that. Maybe it's for dominance. The lambs will basically play a version of the "king of the hill" game. They'll try to get another lamb off the rock by mounting them and making them fall down.

One thing I'm really curious about is intersex animals. I remember meeting a yearling sheep in my first year of fieldwork. My supervisor told me that it was a ram, and I never second-guessed it, because of how the horns looked. We named it "White 20." Then, the next spring, the animal was past its first year and could start giving birth. My boss asked me if I'd seen whether White 20 had a lamb, and I was like, "I thought White 20 was male?" And she replied, "No, when we collared her, she was a female." Phenotypically,* she did look more male. I remember writing in my journal that she was often on the periphery with other yearling rams. Behaviorally she was like them, but then in later years she started to have lambs. I've worked with an intersex mountain goat, too. It was a relocation project, and they thought they'd captured a billy, based on its size, but when they brought the goat back to the station to be processed, they realized it had female and male sex organs. There was some debate about whether to go ahead with the relocation, because it probably wouldn't reproduce.

I'm interested in general in nonprocreative sexualities or asexuality. Sometimes there are sheep that are just . . . not into it? Is there free will in it? Are there sheep that just . . . don't want to breed? It's a hard question to ask, scientifically, but you could start by determining how many females simply aren't breeding with rams.

ELIOT: That question requires giving animals some subjectivity, which science has a hard time with.

LOGAN: Typically, the line of thought is that if females don't breed, it's because they're not in estrus. And if they're not in estrus, it's because they're possibly

---

* *Phenotype* is the physical appearance of an organism, as opposed to *genotype*, which refers to its genetics.

nutritionally limited. But there could be more to it than just that. It would also be worth looking at what's going on from the male side of things, but more difficult because social hierarchies play a role in who gets to breed.

ELIOT: How do your various identities impact you as a scientist?

LOGAN: I'm very open about my identity when it is safe. I was born female, in terms of sex assigned at birth. That's how I was socialized, too, but I wasn't really gender conforming. It's complicated, though: I remember in elementary school that I was obsessed with animals and nature, and especially identified with female teachers who were scientific. Those teachers made me feel okay being myself. During puberty I wasn't happy in my body, and I realized that I wasn't having crushes on guys. I did come out as being gay (or lesbian), for about a year. But when I went on the internet and looked up what the *T* in LGBT means, I realized that I thought I was transgender. It felt right, but then having to tell people about it was scary, so it took me a long time to come out. After my freshman year of college I finally transitioned, switched my pronouns to he/him, and I had top surgery and hormone treatments, because the physical part is probably the main challenge for me.

But because of my history in terms of growing up as female, and who my mentors were, and my socialization, it was hard to lose that part of my history. Some of the people I used to be close with grew apart from me, because people really do see gender. It changes how they interact. I stopped taking hormones and I changed my pronouns back to she/her for a while. It's in a back-and-forth. I feel happier when I put the physical changes I need before the social considerations. I stick with he/him now, because that's how I most often get read and I work in a rural place where passing can actually be a safety factor.

ELIOT: How has it impacted your scientific work?

LOGAN: A lot of my fieldwork is solo, which means I spend time with the animals totally by myself, and not being judged. When I'm watching animals, I can go sunrise to sunset and not take my face away from the scope for hours. It's also really strenuous, physical work. When I'm out there, I'm not thinking about my thoughts or other people or society—I'm more concerned about how I get past a muddy road, or a certain switchback. I love it.

ELIOT: Any advice you'd give to young readers?

LOGAN: Don't be afraid to reach out to biologists, after you've read their book or a paper. A lot of my opportunities started that way, just by expressing interest, being persistent and enthusiastic. Don't feel like you have to follow the expected path, to earn a lot of money and get married, etc. You get to make your own way.

WANT TO LEARN MORE?

Logan is the coauthor (with E. F. Cassirer, G. E. Kaufman, and T. E. Besser) of "*Mycoplasma ovipneumoniae* Strains associated with Pneumonia Outbreaks in North American Bighorn Sheep" in *Biennial Symposium of the Northern Wild Sheep and Goat Council* 20 (2016): 89–97.

Ducks and Geese

WHAT'S THE ANIMAL STANCE ON POLYAMORY?

There's plenty of group sex in the animal world. Bonobos will have an orgy as casually as they'll have breakfast—actually, they'll often have orgies before breakfast! One of my favorite examples of animal group sex (this is not a sentence I ever thought I'd write) is the wolf spider. Like in many spider species, the large female wolf spiders will try to eat the male right after he's mated with her. To help avoid this outcome, a male will sneak into a mating in progress between a female and a male, get it on while the female is distracted by trying to eat the first male, and hightail it out of there. Interestingly enough, the body of the female wolf spider sets this event up perfectly, as it is shaped to allow simultaneous mating from two males. So three-ways most likely have a long-standing role in the evolutionary history of the wolf spider.

Beyond group sex, though, are there polyamorous (multiple-partner) relationships in the animal world?

The answer is yes. Before I go into the whos and the whys, I'm going to tell you a little story about myself that I think illustrates why this question matters.

Clearwater, Florida, where I spent my teenage years, is a pretty good microcosm of the country as a whole: nearly split between Democrat and Republican, a base of progressive younger residents meeting waves of conservative folk retiring and moving down from the Midwest and Canada.

I'm sure there were other queer people in my high school, but they (like me) weren't out. Given how much flak I got in the hallways for being even possibly gay, I wasn't about to come out and take away all doubt. I just didn't feel safe enough.

My mom had a friend through her writer's group, Kathi, who was very cool. She had the sides of her head shaved, she wore men's Bermuda shorts, she had cartilage piercings, she wrote haiku. Her little ranch house near the railroad track was painted peach and was full of her oil paintings and watercolors. She had a big family, with some children she'd given birth to and some she'd adopted, and lots of grandchildren and nieces who were always dropping in for an hour or a week or a year. I never knew who I was going to meet when I went over.

I was writing my first attempt at a novel (an epic fantasy with lots of glowing blue swords in it), and she'd help me with it on Saturday mornings, going through my pages with me and pressing a tome by Tolkien or Eddings or Le Guin into my hands as I left. As I headed out the door, I'd look around to see if I couldn't glimpse one of Kathi's husbands.

Yep, there were two. Roy was a local firefighter, and I heard a total of fifty words come out of his mouth in all the years I was around him. He'd be watching TV if he was home, or smoking out back on the pool lounger. The other husband, Teddy, was a lifeguard at the local rec center, with a big beard and a rosy, impossibly smooth face. He'd often return home from the rec center during our writing sessions, hair still wet from the pool, smelling slightly of chlorine.

I'd met them all when I was a kid, and by the time I had enough knowledge of the world to ask, "hey wait, are they a threesome," it was too late to pose the question. I wasn't really thinking about it, anyway. They were just Kathi and Roy and Teddy, as simple as that. (Thruple wasn't even a word yet, as far as I knew.)

When I once casually mentioned them to some friends, I assumed it would be no big deal. But it was a record-scratch moment. *Wait, what? Who's married to whom? Who's the father of the kids? Do they all have sex? Do the guys kiss? Is it even legal?* I didn't know the answers to those questions. I honestly hadn't felt a need to have an answer to those questions. Since I knew them all pretty well at that point, it kind of didn't matter. Kathi's editing my pages with me, Teddy's whiffs of chlorine, Roy's smoking out back . . . those all seemed more important than the dynamics of what they did in the bedroom. Much bigger on my mind was that I was getting my learner's permit, and I hoped Roy would let me borrow his truck. It was a cool truck.

At the same time, I was feeling a deep hunger to get away from Clearwater, Florida. I knew, clearly and sharply, that I was attracted to men. I also knew that many of the people around me in Tampa Bay called men like me faggots. Kids—friends of mine—would cheerfully say at lunch that all gay people should be rounded up and sent to some island and left to die. Teachers who everyone suspected were gay were fired once the truth came out for sure. I was ready to get out, to go somewhere more accepting.

I had all of high school to get through first, though, so I became a fantasy writer in more ways than one. I was writing a book about elves and fireballs, but I was also spending my shifts at the grocery store fantasizing about the people who came through my line, dreaming up what my future life might look like if I ripped off my Kash n' Karry apron and ran away to live with them.

I knew one thing for sure: Conventionality seemed like the worst thing I could imagine. Conventionality seemed deadly to gay people. As in, conventional people literally wanted us dead. I wanted to question everything about the way the world was structured, break it all down and rebuild it in ways that didn't hate people like me.

I had some female friends that I was low-key out to, and we'd go clubbing on the weekends. We went only to gay nights: my friends because the dancing was better and they didn't have to worry about being hit on, me because I was trying on my future life for a few hours. I was desperate for one of the guys in the club to talk to me, and terrified that they would. Part of trying on that life meant I got my ear pierced at two a.m., that I drew and redrew tattoo designs that I never got. I would lurk through the "gay and lesbian" section of the local bookstore, pulling books at random off the shelf to read in safety on the floor of the self-help section, learning about queer lives lived in other times and other places.

After reading and rereading a couple of swoony gay romances that I kept hidden under my bed, I decided that hearts were generally pulled toward monogamy, but that rigid, externally imposed monogamy was a trap. If a heart wanted to stray for a while, then shouldn't we let it? What was that popular phrase, after all: "If you truly love something, set it free"? I told myself that otherwise we'd be limiting the potential of our capacity to love, and we only have one life on this planet, so shouldn't we experience as much as we could? I also wondered: maybe fewer couples would ever need to break up if they felt permitted to act on sexual desire outside the relationship. (My parents were heading for divorce after my dad had an affair.)

Here's the future I kept going to in my mind as I bagged people's groceries at the Kash n' Karry, dreaming of hopping in their car with them and hightailing it out of Clearwater: I'd live in a narrow, sweet, rickety town house in San Francisco, Atlanta, Brooklyn. I'd have a partner named Darius who, I don't know, made pottery and liked to surprise me with weekend trips to go hiking and collect bluebells. We'd settle in that house with two women, also in a relationship, and the four of us would raise kids, all combinations of mothers and fathers, someone always home to take care of the little ones, each having dinner duty a couple nights a week, a huddle of loving and hard-to-define people. A community as well as a family.

I realize now that it was also a perfectly closeted-not-closeted life that I'd dreamed up for myself. Everyone in the house would be gay, but the realtor, the neighbor, the electrician, might think we were two straight couples living together. I could have my gay life and not worry about being called a faggot, all at once. Even as I dreamed big, I was still living in the hangover of the homophobia of my surroundings.

It would take leaving Clearwater for good, and spending years around friends who were queer or queer-friendly, for me to process most of that internalized homophobia out of my system. Not that a shared house with multiple other people wouldn't have been a great idea if the opportunity came along . . . but I'd definitely want to know how much my experience of being closeted had to do with that fantasy. By the time I was through college, and much more comfortable in my own skin, I found it had become just fine if the realtor, the neighbor, the electrician knew I was with another guy.

I'm a brain-first and heart-second kind of person, so I also assumed that this capacity to live a life that wasn't preordained, that was on my own terms, would take some mental heavy lifting. That every instinct and all my cultural conditioning would push me toward the conventional, but if I thought long and hard enough I'd be able to strip that away and live a less traditional existence.

Underlying that all was the assumption that the natural world was either about heterosexual partnership (like two swans on a lake raising their young), single parenting (like Charlotte caring for her egg clutch while she chatted with Wilbur), or absent parenting (like a sea turtle laying eggs, never to check on the hatchlings).

Meanwhile, as you've seen in the previous chapters, it turns out I was wrong in that assumption. There's a huge diversity in who's shacking up with whom in the animal world. Lots of animals are not monogamous, not even a bit, and other animals never have sex, and there's everything in between. There's also plenty of homosexual coupling and bonding.

But are there bonded groups, like Kathi and Teddy and Roy?

Yes.

Lots. They're mostly in birds.

It's not easy being a bird. Think about it: you're a delicious plump creature, and because your young are stuck in eggs and can't move, you're trapped in one place too. This makes bird parents especially vulnerable to predators. If you're a cricket, say, you can lay your eggs and book it out of there. If you're a mammal, you can carry your developing young in your womb, so you can run from predators while they're growing. Your offspring emerge fully formed, walking around and able to flee danger within minutes. (Humans are

a notable exception. We give birth to positively useless newborns that we have to haul around for months before they can even take a step.)

If a snake or a fox comes by, bird parents can't just leave. They have to stay and fight. This leads to high levels of mortality in nesting birds, especially among females (who do the greater share of the nest guarding). The only option other than being a literal sitting duck is to leave the nest unguarded for periods, which makes those little eggs prime pickings—or vulnerable to competitive neighbors. Gulls, especially, will regularly go smash up the unattended eggs of other gulls.

Not cool.

Might it not be useful, then, to have more than two parents in the household?

One very highly studied bird species is the greylag goose (not to be confused with Grey Goose, which is a highly studied brand of vodka). One group of greylag geese has been observed for generations, allowing scientists to track individuals over many years. It's only in this unusual sort of longitudinal study that an animal's long-term relationship patterns emerge. The researchers also used advances in DNA testing to determine who the parents were for various eggs in nests, and came up with some surprising results.

For starters, turns out there is a ton of extramarital canoodling among greylag geese. Even for a straight-up heterosexual goose couple, there's a good chance that their gosling was fathered by some goose outside the union. This is an important distinction: more than 90 percent of bird species are *socially* monogamous, meaning the birds choose one partner, only finding another if the first dies or disappears, but *genetic* monogamy occurs in only 25 percent of bird species. In other words, most birds have what humans would call open relationships. They're committed to one partner, often for life, but still have sex on the side.

In the geese, upward of 10 percent of their nests are cared for by thruples instead of couples. Most often these threesomes are composed of two males and a female, though female-female-male thruples do occur. With three parents, the eggs have a much better chance of surviving. As researcher Philippe Carruette put it, "The advantage for a trio is quite obvious . . . each bird has in effect three birds to look after its chicks . . . also, since the female is with two males she has a higher social rank and a better chance of survival. The female also has more time to take care of the chicks and then seek food for herself." While only about 20 percent of heterosexual pairs manage to raise young to fledging, the rates are higher for these three-goose nests.

Geese and swans and ducks go through elaborate romance rituals that put our prom corsages and boutonnieres to shame. If a bird wants to successfully woo, they have to hold their head the right way, make the right squawks, do the right dances. It's like they're in some king's court, where achievement depends on showing subservience and dominance to the right people in just the right way.

For greylag geese, one of the most important rituals is called the triumph ceremony. It's all blustery and macho and frat-y. In order to show off, a male will leave the nest and go pick a fight with a nearby male. The fight might be a real combat, with nipping and biting, or just a big show of charging and trumpeting and clacking beaks. Then he struts back to his nest, all proud of himself. That's when the sounds change. He sticks out his chest and his voice goes soft, and he snuggles for a while with his partner(s). Basically, he goes and pretends to fight a stranger, then comes back and says, "Baby, baby, look how I protect you, don't you love me?"

The triumph ceremony is important to greylag society because it helps define the goose family group by announcing to the other geese that they are a unit. It works sort of like conspicuous wedding rings, or wearing a boyfriend/girlfriend's sweatshirt, declaring to the outside world that these geese are a thing, so don't butt in.

Important for us in this book is that, when geese are in a thruple, a male will go pick a fight, then return and perform the ceremony to both his partners, the male and the female. It's just as important that he announce his union with the other male as with the female. The goose thruples aren't just about group sex, or tolerating the presence of another bird for only a short time (like we saw with the albatrosses of chapter 8, when females invite a male in only as long as it takes to mate). For the geese, this thruple is the real deal. A three-person relationship.

Sometimes a female will return to the same male couple season after season, the three of them raising many goslings together. Other times the male partners will stay the same, but they'll choose a new female for the next season, particularly if the previous year's thruple didn't produce any surviving offspring.

As we've seen over and over, the general rule in the animal world is that bisexuality is far more common than homosexuality. But there are, in fact, some "gay" greylag geese. By the accounting of the foremost study site, roughly half of the males were exclusively hetero in their mate choice, a third chose a mixture of males and females over time, and the remainder were exclusively homosexual. It's not just that these males occasionally had sex with males; they could actually be said to have a homosexual orientation, meaning an exclusive interest in courting and bonding with other males.

Though greylag geese don't tend to form exclusive female-female bonds, there are many other bird species that do, like the pukeko, Eurasian oystercatcher, gulls, and terns. And ducks. In autumn, some female mallard ducks will perform what's known as the "pumping" display, a prelude to mating, and then will copulate with another female. They'll have sex with other females even though they're paired with a male, or they'll bond with the female, forming a same-sex union.

A lot of birds (like the Edinburgh penguins we met in the introduction) are difficult to sex, and for a long time observers would make assumptions about who was male and who was female purely based on their behavior. Now that we can determine a bird's sex using a blood sample, we realize that these hetero assumptions were often wrong. Nobel Prize–winning ornithologist Konrad Lorenz recounts an amusing story about a parrot breeder who for a long time would put two birds together and identify which was male and which was female by who was "dominant" or "passive" in their courtship—only to realize once they started laying eggs that his sex IDs were all scrambled. Turned out that it was simply the second bird placed in the cage that took on the "submissive" sexual role, probably because they sensed they were entering the first bird's territory. The pair could be two males, a male and a female, or two females. Same goes for grouse and pigeons; even expert pigeon breeders won't realize they have two females as their breeding pair until they find four eggs in the nest instead of two. Often those eggs will be fertilized, as the females might have had sex with males. But the partnership is between females.

The simplest mechanism of evolution is selection on the individual level (i.e., "survival of the fittest," in which the individual with the longest life and the most offspring passes the most genes to the next generation). There are good reasons for polyamory to evolve on the level of individual selection since, like in the case of the greylag geese, three birds might produce more surviving young by increasing the number of parents tending the nest.

But polyamory might also help on the level of *group* selection, increasing the survivability of the population as a whole. When males shack up, they tend to make a lot more noise and ruckus than male-female couples do. They're also more aggressive toward external threats and will be more likely to come to the defense of the whole area if a predator comes near. Interestingly enough, these male unions, with a female added seasonally to become a threesome, also tend to settle their nests on the edge of the flock. They're at higher risk of being eaten this way, which decreases their individual fitness, but by serving as the warrior defenders of the group, they help everyone survive. This has led some researchers to propose that perhaps male homosexual bonding has been evolutionarily selected to produce built-in guardians for all the birds in the area.

When creatures like birds have social monogamy but not genetic monogamy,  it means that bisexuality doesn't result in lower numbers of offspring, so there's no reason for evolution to select against it. The "male protectors" argument forms a pretty good adaptive explanation for homosexual bonding in birds. It's similar to arguments that same-sex partnering in animals might produce a built-in foster parent system into populations. They're both pleasing explanatory stories . . . but evolutionary biologists often rightly roll their eyes about these compelling but unproven just-so stories of why something evolved. Evolution is often more complicated than any simple explanation. More research is needed, but even after that occurs, we might ultimately have to allow that polyamory in animals, like in humans, simply *is*, and doesn't need a tidy origin story.

There are lots of human sexual behaviors for which we don't feel the need to come up with evolutionary explanations, and we ought to extend animals the same leeway. However, that doesn't mean we can't use our knowledge of human emotions to help us understand how and why animals might behave the way they do. We too are animals, after all. As Charles Darwin himself put it, "The difference in mind between man and the higher animals, great as it is, certainly is one of degree and not of kind."

Science as we commonly think of it requires making a prediction and then testing that prediction. The testing can be done through reasoning and experimentation. The prediction part, though, often must come from our intuitive understanding of animal behavior, because of our own emotional lives as animals. There has to be a place for that in science, too. As Konrad Lorenz writes, "Both aspects, intuitive understanding and scientific knowledge, are needed to give us the ability to make predictions . . . the extensive and quantifiable analogies that exist between the behavioral systems of greylag geese and those of humans strongly argue that they have arisen through phylogenetic convergence under the influence of similar selection pressures." In other words, if your gut tells you that a bird's impulse toward polyamory might be similar to the human one, that's a valid starting point for a scientific investigation.

I love hearing about these bird thruples, mainly because a lot of our human assumptions around polyamory are that it's naive and doomed to fail. People will get jealous, the thinking goes, and it's best just to settle down with one person because "it's the way it's meant to be." For many of us, though, that's just not how our hearts are constructed, and we can do ourselves a lot of harm by trying to bully ourselves into behaving the way society wants us to. Lots of humans pretend at monogamy and then go around cheating in secret (i.e., more of us than we know practice social but not genetic monogamy).

The dishonesty element in the human version harms the partner that's being lied to, and it harms the cheating individual, who now has to live with the stress of a secret. (Not to mention the complications of STDs and neglected or secret offspring, etc.) What if people drawn to polyamory could form unions where they didn't have to go around lying about it? Even though doing so isn't conventional in Western society, it's possible to have an openly polyamorous union that's sustainable in the long term. Ducks and geese and swans show that to be true.

Of course, there are forms of human polyamory, like our long history of powerful older men taking on multiple younger wives who have little say in the matter, that feel coercive and unjust. But I think sometimes of that town-house fantasy I had when I was younger, of multiple couples living entangled lives together. I'd discarded that thought quickly. I wonder, though, as I read about animal polyamory in the natural world . . . how many of my assumptions about what a "good relationship" looks like are just the result of stories I've internalized, rather than any objective truth? Did I just assume that any polyamorous relationship is doomed because I didn't see many? All I'd seen of polyamory was Kathi and Teddy and Roy, and as far as teenage me knew, they were the only people in the world who lived the way they did. What if there were more examples of it, if polyamory were positively portrayed in the books I read in school, on television, in our communities and our politics? In science? Maybe some human thruples are doomed only because all three parties went into it assuming the relationship was doomed.

The greylag goose flock is protected by the aggressive male-male-female trios at its edge, and all the little goslings have extra parents to care for them. This sounds like something to admire, not to fear. Evolutionary biologists might say that "polyamory in birds produces a union in which everyone's fitness benefits." A goose has a subjective experience of that, though, and isn't thinking about evolutionary reasons for what they're doing. We could just as easily think of this as a case of a goose choosing the nestmates they want for themself. How wonderful that the geese live in a society where no one gives a flying feather whether a nest has two or three (or sometimes four!) birds caring for it. They're onto the much more important business of keeping eggs warm and getting enough sweet grasses to eat.

I had Kathi read this chapter, and then asked her if she had any words to share about her life with Teddy and Roy. She told me that some people embraced them unconditionally, and some cut them out of their lives. She thinks their union was more threatening to those people because she and Teddy and Roy were happy. "If we had been miserable some would have forgiven us." As for their kids, they were in full support, because it meant that someone was always home for them.

Dylan Sanborn

(EDITED FOR LENGTH AND CLARITY)

NAME: **DYLAN SANBORN**
PRONOUNS: **HE/HIS**
INSTAGRAM: **@HIKINGBIRD**
JOB: **WILDLIFE TECHNICIAN / AVIAN BIOLOGIST**

ELIOT: What's been the role of wildlife in your life?

DYLAN: Ever since I was a kid I knew I wanted to work with animals, but didn't really know what route to go down. I had a very outdoorsy mom, and we would go hiking all the time. At Colorado State University, I started pursuing my zoology degree, because I was thinking about going into veterinary sciences. But then I learned about field biology and I was pretty much hooked. My first job was doing rehab work with different raptor species. I've worked in Hawaii, Georgia, and Minnesota, but for three seasons I've been at Yellowstone. In the winter I work with the wolf program, and the rest of the year I'm with birds.

ELIOT: What draws you to birds?

DYLAN: I love the sheer diversity. There are eleven thousand estimated bird species worldwide. In Yellowstone there are about three hundred species that we work with. Personally, too, I consider myself somewhat of an ecologist, and bird health is so deeply related to the health of their habitat; it's nice to see the ecological connections.

ELIOT: Are you collecting data that's for use in science further down the road, or are you targeting environmental or conservation issues that are impacting the animal in the here and now?

DYLAN: When we're looking at say, raptors, we're monitoring them within the greater Yellowstone ecosystem. We also want to get better population estimates of those species as a whole. That's very useful, especially for some species like the bald eagle or peregrine falcon, whose populations were heavily suppressed in the past by pollutants like DDT. Now we can see that they've actually been increasing, at least in this part. That helps with conservation efforts in the future.

ELIOT: Does the concept of same-sex sexual behavior in birds come up in your work life, or have you observed it?

DYLAN: There are 130 different bird species on the record as having same-sex behaviors. They'll engage in same-sex behaviors as far as courtship or mating. So there's evidence of it, and I find it fascinating, but I haven't seen it in Yellowstone, or it hasn't been researched here.

ELIOT: Is it difficult to sex the birds that you're treating, or is it clear who's male and who's female?

DYLAN: It's very dependent. There are some species where, due to plumage, you can tell if they're male or female. Or you can tell by the brood patch for some species, because in some it's the females who will incubate eggs.

ELIOT: How have your own personal identifications impacted your work?

DYLAN: I use he/him pronouns and identify as gay. Some parts are difficult, like dating or being able to find other people that are in the gay community. My boyfriend and I, we've talked about how it can be hard to find people in the LGBTQ community, but we kind of lucked out. We're both wildlife biologists. It's great being in wildlife conservation because you also work around people who tend to be very progressive, with a very high level of acceptance for people like myself.

ELIOT: It does feel like the more you spend time in nature, it brings about this radical acceptance and empathy. Everything just *is*.

DYLAN: Yeah, I aim to bring visibility to people in the science and wildlife community who are gay or in the LGBTQ community. This field is not just for people who are hetero or cisgender. This field is really for anyone.

ELIOT: Anything you'd like young readers to know?

DYLAN: Let's say you're talking about birds in class. You could go out and look for them. I think a lot of people experience this disconnect, because they read the textbook but don't think about practical field applications. If I were a ninth grader learning about biology, I would go for a hike. If you're going out in the field, it makes you want to read more about animals in the classroom and then, when you read more about them in the classroom, you want to go back out into the field.

WANT TO LEARN MORE?

Learn about science and research happening at Yellowstone: www.nps.gov/yell/learn /scienceresearch.htm.

Check out Dylan's amazing wildlife photography at fineartamerica.com/profiles/dylan -sanborn.

CONCLUSION

HAS ANYONE ASKED THOSE PENGUINS THEIR TAKE ON ALL THIS?

It's not that creatures work as models for human lives—no one I know thinks that humans should spawn like wave-borne fish or subsist entirely on flies— but the more I've learned about animals the more I've come to think there might not be only one right way to express care, to feel allegiance, a love for place, a way of moving through the world. —Helen MacDonald, Vesper Flights

We're creations of our culture. Even those of us who fight to reform and progress, to improve the world we're born into, are still stamped by the civilization that made us. For those of us who grew up in places dominated by the Abrahamic religious worldviews—Judaism, Christianity, and Islam—one of those entrenched biases is human exceptionalism. Also known as human supremacy or anthropocentrism, it's the belief that we're the most important beings in the universe.

According to Genesis in the Bible, for example, God made humans on a separate day from all the rest of creation, and called upon them to "Be fruitful, and multiply, and replenish the earth, and subdue it: and have dominion over the fish of the sea, and over the fowl of the air, and over every living thing that moveth upon the earth" (King James Version).* In the Koran, humans are

---

* There's been a lot of debate about the translation of "dominion," which might call on us to be "stewards" of the natural world more than "rulers." That humans are given agency over the natural world is uncontestable, however. For more on Christian animal welfare worldviews, focusing on our moral obligation to practice mercy, check out Matthew Scully's compelling book *Dominion: The Power of Man, the Suffering of Animals, and the Call to Mercy.*

similarly on the top of a hierarchy, above other animals and plants.

Human exceptionalism tells us that we are different from all other animals by our sacred nature. It tells us that we are the only creatures with souls, and that a human life is worth more than any number of animal lives. It tells us that it is intellectually wrongheaded in the sciences to anthropomorphize, or assign human qualities to nonhuman animals. That has effectively allowed scientists to avoid assigning *any* emotions to their animal subjects.

When she began to study wild chimpanzees in the 1960s, Jane Goodall was ridiculed in the scientific academy for giving her subjects names like Frodo and Fifi, though she credits that naming with allowing her to see them as individuals with their own drives and desires—and therefore to observe a greater range of behaviors within them. (One of Goodall's chimpanzees, Flo, became so beloved by the reading public that she is the only nonhuman ever to receive an obituary in the *Sunday Times*.)

Human exceptionalism tells us that the land and its inhabitants were placed here for us to use, that they are property and "natural resources" rather than beings with internal lives and identities. Human exceptionalism allows hunting without consuming what's hunted, allows raising animals in horrific factory farms where the press is legally forbidden to go, through "ag-gag" laws. It allows pricking a bull, making him charge to prove how brave the toreador is, and then slaying him.

Although human exceptionalism is still going strong, it has also taken some big hits since the days of Genesis. Maybe the biggest was when Charles Darwin published his theory of evolution by natural selection, which compellingly argued that humans and apes share a common ancestor. It's hard to overstate how shocking that would have been to a world that truly saw humans as something separate from the rest of creation. Humans couldn't be related to animals! We had *souls*, for the love of God! We were created on an entirely different day! Darwin's science showed that humans shared their family tree with other animals—and that therefore the creatures around us are relatives, not objects for us to use at will.

Human exceptionalism is a fancy pair of words, but we inherited the instinct it describes from our animal ancestors. As our chimp and bonobo cousins tell us (remember, they share nearly 99 percent of our DNA), we are creatures dominated by in-group/out-group behavior. Consciously and unconsciously, we value what we see as "our people" and devalue what we identify as "other." This is not always an intellectual choice, though sometimes prejudice can reveal itself through our active choices. It's hardwired in us, through our systems of oxytocin bonding and group survival. For the millions of years during which our brains evolved, our main focus was keeping the sixteen or so individuals around us alive, and outcompeting the group that was on the other side of the hill, even if they had just as much of a right to live. Even if they were apes like us.

This yearning to belong to a group, and to forbid inclusion to outsiders, is deep in the hardwiring of our brains. It has led to all sorts of injustices over the years, like the dehumanizing of foreign peoples that led to slavery and genocides. Less dramatically, this human tribalism leads to sports-team loyalties that boil into bloodshed, or to adherence to a political belief system that sees the other side as so "evil" that murder is a fair recourse. As science historian Beans Velocci (see Q&A, page 100) put it, this time in the context of a move under the Trump administration to "essentially classify transgender and intersex people out of existence," we have "a long history of hiding violent and exclusionary policy behind claims about the natural order of things."

Our language is a prime example. What we speak about, and how we speak about it, is a road map to what's important to us—to what we treasure and what we disregard. The way we describe animals is especially telling. As Indigenous botanist Robin Wall Kimmerer writes in her book *Braiding Sweetgrass*:

> *Imagine seeing your grandmother standing at the stove in her apron and then saying of her, "Look, it is making soup. It has gray hair." We might snicker at such a mistake, but we also recoil from it . . . It robs a person of selfhood and kinship, reducing a person to a mere thing.*

Animals are reduced by the pronouns we use for them, when they become "it" instead of "he" or "she" or "they." I've always found it interesting that pets manage to get human pronouns, but they're pretty much the only animals that do. Mr. Mittens is a "he," but the mouse he's chasing across the floor, and the squirrel watching from outside the window, are each "it." For the most part, so are the animals that are the subjects of scientific study.

Kimmerer learned her tribe's language as an adult and came to important scientific realizations in her work as a botanist from the worldview embedded in the Potawatomi language. Personhood is given freely to plants and animals through the language itself.

Changing the words we use doesn't just alter the way we speak. It also alters the way we think. Kimmerer notes that she not only made important scientific discoveries by relying on her Indigenous background; she also found comfort. Separating ourselves from the animal world might give us a lot of power, but it also gives us a weight to bear, removes an important way to feel connected to the larger web of existences around us:

Learning the grammar of animacy could well be a restraint on our mindless exploitation of land. But there is more to it. . . . Imagine the access we would have to different perspectives, the things we might see through other eyes, the wisdom that surrounds us. We don't have to figure out everything by ourselves: there are intelligences other than our own, teachers all around us. Imagine how less lonely the world would be.

You might be thinking it's been a while since I talked about queer animals. But it's not, really. I think it's no coincidence that the Indigenous worldview that reclaims animals as our brethren is also the same one that valued queer people long before there were gay rights movements, long before the word *homosexual* (or *heterosexual*, for that matter) even existed.

The umbrella term North American Indigenous people use to describe people who would otherwise be called LGBTQIAP+ is *two-spirit* (i.e., both male and female spirits within one body). It's a recent coinage, coming from the 1990 Indigenous lesbian and gay international gathering, as a way to describe people who have many different names in the various tribal languages. Since North American Indigenous languages are more verb-focused than noun-focused, there aren't identity-based terms in most cultures (similar to the ancient human cultures described in chapter 4), and *two-spirit* was settled on as a way to describe a diversity of gender expressions and sexual/social roles for outside audiences. (Even *two-spirit* doesn't sit right with some native thinkers, who feel it has the potential to reduce the diversity of native sexualities into one Westernized pot and reinforces the binary of male/female.)

The homophobia present in our society, coupled with the human exceptionalism that makes us resist seeing the personhood or subjectivity of animals, has led to a double disregard of, or in some cases aggressive attacks against, animal queerness in the field.

One reason why queer animal behavior is missing from your average high school textbook (or in the broader scientific literature, for that matter) is that the academic study of science is generally species-based. A biologist typically becomes an expert in one animal, studies that animal, writes their dissertation on that animal. That dissertation contributes to the published research on that creature, and is also what gets that young scientist their first academic job. Is queer behavior in that dissertation? Probably not. Since they're not going into the field looking for queer behavior, they simply might not see it, assuming any mating animals they see are male and female. If they do bother to sex the animals they see mating, and discover queerness in their species, they might assume that it's from an error in their observations, or that it's a peculiarity limited to that population.

Even if they do think it's of interest, young scientists might be reluctant to publish it. Articles undergo what's called peer review, in which leading experts in the field assess the scientific validity of a paper's claims. Say you're a twentysomething studying geckos, and the six hundred pages of scientific literature that currently exist on geckos, published by giants in the field, don't mention any homosexual behavior. You *saw* it, though! You could bravely write on that finding, contradicting your immediate adviser, and the professors who are in charge of your academic future, and risk established scientists writing to the journal to complain that your upstart study contradicts their own well-accepted studies . . . or you could decide to publish on some other aspect of gecko behavior.

If you want to get a job and pay your bills, wouldn't it be easier to just publish on foraging strategies instead of homosexuality? Everyone loves foraging strategies. No one writes hate mail about foraging strategies. So, you make that reluctant choice. Your queer-erasing article comes out. Now there are 620 pages of scientific literature on geckos that don't mention homosexual behavior. There's even more precedent discouraging young and unestablished researchers from going against the flow.

It's all pretty similar to what it's like in times and locations where everyone with queer feelings stays closeted. Everyone assumes they're the only one, that no one else is like this, when there might be queer people all around, too afraid to reveal themselves.

Another reason for the lack of publishing on queer animals is the homophobia in our society. When young graduate student Linda Wolfe first published on the frequent female-female sexual activity between Japanese macaques in the 1970s, she expected the scientific community to be excited that she had made a new discovery, had taken an important step forward in the study of primates. It didn't go that way: "People started to ask me, do you have some kinky interest we don't know about? . . . They said that females were mounting each other by mistake—they didn't know what they were doing. People wanted to believe that only weirdo humans engaged in this behavior."

Same-sex sexual behavior, Wolfe notes, "is normal . . . part of what primates do, part of their total sexual repertoire." And not just primates, of course, as we've seen. The number of species with confirmed substantial queer behaviors, published in well-regarded scientific journals, is 1,500 and growing.

Tellingly, for two of the most prominent books on queer animal behavior, *Biological Exuberance* by Bruce Bagemihl and *Homosexual Behaviour in Animals* by Volker Sommer and Paul L. Vasey, the authors' methodology was to approach researchers who had preexisting study sites and data sets on animals and ask them if they had observed same-sex behaviors in their study animals that they hadn't published. The answers were resoundingly "yes." For species after species, the observations of queer behavior were there—they just weren't being printed.

As we've seen, there's vigorous debate on what the evolutionary explanations for queer animals might be—and whether pursuing such explanations is necessary or useful. It turns out that there isn't one blanket reason for why queerness is so prevalent in the animal world. Sometimes it might be to provide social glue for a relationship, as in the bottlenose dolphins or black swans (or many human societies), in which males form a dominating union through their sexual activity. Maybe it's to minimize conflict and tension within the group, as in the bonobos. Maybe it's out of evolved lack of discrimination, so no mating opportunity is missed, as in the doodlebugs. Maybe sexual expression changes according to a changing social environment, as in the wrasse fish. Maybe polyamory makes for safer chicks, like in the greylag geese. Maybe courtship and lifetime pair bonding occur between females that have heterosexual sex outside the union, like in the albatross. Maybe sexual expression lives outside of a two-sex binary from birth, as in the case of the velvet-horn deer.

Or maybe, as in the case of the penguins and the Japanese macaques, the most reasonable conclusion is that they're doing it simply because they want to.

Only a few animal species appear to have members who have persistent same-sex orientations. With no value judgments or cultural prohibitions blocking nonhuman animals from pursuing it, bisexuality flourishes in the animal world. Sexual fluidity increases the sheer quantity of sex that occurs within a species as a whole, which has an evolutionary benefit. As the study Max Lambert (see Q&A on page 114) coauthored in *Scientific American* put it, an "ancestral condition of indiscriminate sexual behaviors directed towards all sexes"—that is, bisexuality as the essential norm throughout the tree of life, not heterosexuality—incurs little cost to a species' fitness. Eggs will still be fertilized, young will still be raised, while animals can also reap the benefits of the bonding and socializing produced by queer behaviors. Bonus: they also experience sexual pleasure more often. Bisexual Advantage isn't just a cool band name—it just might be a guiding principle in the history of life.

Maybe animals engaging in queer sex can just enjoy the sexual responses that evolved for heterosexual intercourse, with no evolutionary purpose for the same-sex act. As Paul Vasey (see Japanese macaque discussion in chapter 5) notes, "researchers have been blinded by the prevailing preoccupation to find adaptive explanations for every behavior." He turns to the example of a macaque troop he studied, in which there were many females and just one male. "Even in that skewed situation, that one male was not very busy. By and large the females were more interested in other females—they're bisexual, not preferentially heterosexual."

Some people (maybe many people) reading this book right now are angry. Many will argue (and have argued) that just because something occurs in the animal world, that doesn't mean that humans ought to do it, too. After all, no one's advocating that human females ought to eat males after having sex with them, like praying mantises do, or that we should have sex on top of corpses or eat our young or cannibalize our parents or any of the other behaviors that are found in the natural world.

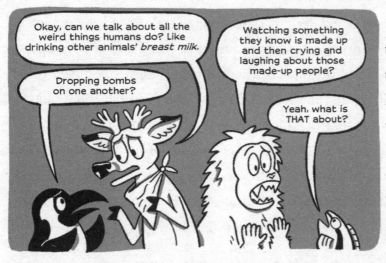

That's taking this book the wrong way. I'm not telling people to go behave like fruit flies. If that's their interpretation, the butt they have their heads up might be their own. This book (like almost all the articles I've read on queer animal behavior) does not try to argue *for* queer human sexuality *from* the example of animals. Instead, it's the reverse: what I am saying is that we can no longer argue that humans are alone in their queerness, that nonheteronormative human sexualities and gender identities are unnatural because they don't exist in the rest of the animal kingdom. That position is simply not valid. Queerness is a well-established and fundamental part of nature. If queerness is "wrong," then you'd better be willing to say that the entire animal kingdom is wrong. In which case—I guess you can go hang out with some bacteria?

Remember the penguins from the intro, when Andrew became Ann, Bertha became Bertrand, Caroline became Charles, and Eric became Erica, and a whole bunch of them turned out to be queer? Ninety-two years after the Edinburgh Zoo was rocked by its first gay penguin sex scandals, the documentary

movie *March of the Penguins* came out in 2005. It told the story of loving heterosexual penguin couples who braved the frigid Antarctic winter to raise their chicks. It was a smash hit. Conservative commentators praised the penguins as pinnacles of traditional family values, upholding the nuclear family. The few people who were aware of the rampant bisexuality in the penguin world wrote opposing opinion pieces, arguing that many of those bird couples presented as straight in the documentary might just as easily have been same-sex. I mean, do *you* know how to tell boy and girl penguins apart?

I think the most compelling argument in response to the film, however, was from biologist Marlene Zuk, who wrote a piece in *Nature* cautioning us to avoid using animals to argue about human morality at all—in either direction. To do so risks making animals symbols instead of subjects, makes them accessories to our selfish interest in humans, in human lives and human dramas. "If we use animals as poster children for ideology," Zuk warns, "we not only end up in meaningless arguments over whose examples are more significant (cannibalistic mantids or promiscuous bonobos?), we risk losing sight of what is truly interesting and important about their behaviour."

While the "why" of animal queerness is still a topic of productive and exciting scientific debate, the "that" of it—the fact that animal queerness exists and is substantially represented in the natural world—is unmistakable. There's an incredible diversity to animal sexual behavior and sexual expression, and each new piece of research in this exciting field has led to revelations that reshape what we assume animals are capable of—and what humans themselves are capable of. Queer behavior in animals is as diverse and complex—and natural—as any other sort of sexual behavior.

It's not the natural order that declares humans as heterosexual until proven otherwise. That's all a product of human culture, and human culture is something that our ancestors made up as they went along. What naysayers call "nature's intention" is just how centuries of humans have decided it ought to be. And there's no need to keep traditions that hurt or exclude anyone. After all, traditions are just peer pressure from dead people. We get to make new ones of our own.

WANT TO READ MORE RIGHT AWAY?

Here are some short sources that are easy entry points into further reading and viewing, suitable for general readers or for classroom use. Full citations can be found in the Selected Bibliography.

"Queer Creatures," Gail Vines, *New Scientist*, 1999.

An engaging, solidly reported, and accessible introduction to the recent growth of research into same-sex sexual behavior in animals.

"Animal Homosexuality" episode, *Animals Like Us*, 2004.

This episode in an otherwise under-the-radar documentary series became a cult phenomenon. Includes plenty of footage of wild same-sex sexual behavior, and interviews with prominent biologists. Also: hilarious pronunciations of the word *homosexual*.

"Family Values in Black & White," Marlene Zuk, *Nature*, 2006.

An evenhanded one-page debate about the reception to the film *March of the Penguins*, ultimately reminding us to keep animals in view, instead of using them as metaphors for human behavior.

"Goslings of Gay Geese," Jared Diamond, *Nature*, 1989.

A brisk and engaging one-page introduction to same-sex parenting in shorebirds.

"Same Sex Behavior and Evolution," Nathan W. Bailey & Marlene Zuk, *Trends in Ecology & Evolution*, 2009.
More advanced but still accessible scholarly survey of queer animal behavior, with lots of sourcing to branch out into researching individual species.

"Why Is Same-Sex Sexual Behavior So Common in Animals?," Ambika Kamath et al., *Scientific American*, 2019.
A public-facing summary of the authors' scholarly article arguing that same-sex sexual behavior is likely to have persisted throughout the history of life, a hypothesis the authors hope "will expand understanding of the diversity of the natural world."

Acknowledgments

I'm so grateful to the scientists and researchers who gave freely of their time so their words could be included in this book's Q&As: Christine Webb, Sidney Woodruff, Mounica Kota, Beans Velocci, Max Lambert, Logan Weyand, and Dylan Sanborn.

One of the greatest things about practicing science is that no one has to start from the beginning. There is absolutely no way this book could have been written without the softened pages of my tattered copy of Bruce Bagemihl's *Biological Exuberance*. He wrote 750 pages of exhaustively researched, fascinating commentary on same-sex sexual behavior in animals. The field of Animal Studies owes him an enormous debt, and so do I.

Thanks to my colleagues in the New York University Animal Studies department, and in particular Jeff Sebo, who read pages for me; Becca Franks, who led me through an independent study on this topic; and Nico Stubler, who is a committed and passionate animal advocate and a wonderful writer to boot.

I'm grateful to Dae C. and Cath for their insights into how my words might affect readers whose identities and backgrounds are different from mine.

My writers group—Daphne Benedis-Grab, Jill Santopolo, Marie Rutkoski, and Marianna Baer—were instrumental in providing feedback, as ever. My mom gave the book a thorough line edit, as did my husband, Eric Zahler. Elana K. Arnold, Donna Freitas, Nicole Mueller, and Emily Greenhill were all important early readers as well.

A hearty thank you to my agent, Richard Pine, and the whole team at Katherine Tegen Books, from design and copyediting through sales and marketing: the queer ducks are lucky to have you on their side. Particular shoutouts to senior production editor Laura Harshberger and copy editor Megan Gendell, school and library mavens Patty Rosati and Mimi Rankin, Mitchell Thorpe in publicity and Michael D'Angelo in marketing, and designer David Curtis.

Extra big thanks to this book's editor, Ben Rosenthal, for his insight, wisdom, and kindness, and to assistant editor Tanu Srivastava.

Jules Zuckerberg, I want to live inside your drawn worlds. Thank you for bringing the animal GSA to life! I just heard from the macaques—you can totally sit with them at lunch.

GLOSSARY

ADAPTATION: In evolutionary biology, refers to a change in a species' lineage that makes it better suited to its environment.

ADAPTIVE: Leading to or resulting from adaptation.

ALLOHORMONE: A hormone transferred between individuals.

ANIMAL: See page 25 ("What Queer Means").

ANTHROPOCENTRISM: The belief that humans are essentially different from, and superior to, other animals. Sometimes called human exceptionalism or human supremacy.

ANTHROPODENIAL: The tendency within the sciences to deny animals mental states that humans also have. (related: anthropomorphism)

ANTHROPOLOGY: The study of human cultures and human evolutionary development.

ANTHROPOMORPHISM: Assigning human feelings or traits to nonhuman entities. (related: anthropodenial)

ASEXUAL: Without feelings of sexual attraction. In biology, also refers to reproducing without sexual activity.

BASE PAIRS: Two nucleotides that come together to form the structure of DNA.

BISEXUAL: Relating to the desire for both one's own and the opposite gender or sex. (related: pansexual)

BOVID: A ruminant vertebrate with cloven hoofs. Includes bison, buffalo, sheep, goats, and cattle.

CAPACITATION: Alteration to sperm within the female reproductive system that allows them to penetrate the egg.

CISGENDER: Describes someone whose personal identity corresponds with their sex assigned at birth. (related: transgender)

CULTURE: The teaching and learning of behavior, between individuals and over generations. Increasingly used in reference to nonhuman animals as well as humans.

DEMISEXUAL: Refers to someone who is sexually attracted only to people they have an emotional bond with.

DIMORPHIC: Displaying in two different forms. (In sexually dimorphic species, males and females have differences in appearance beyond just having different sex organs.)

ENZYME: A substance that helps begin or strengthen a biochemical reaction.

ETHOLOGY: The scientific study of animal behavior.

EVOLUTION, THEORY OF: The idea that all species are related and change over time. (Note: though in everyday speech we use the word *theory* to refer to something that's a hunch, in science it's much the opposite, referring to something—like gravity, which is also a "theory"—that serves to explain and combine many different pieces of evidence from the natural world. If someone tells you "evolution is just a theory," they're using the term incorrectly.)

FELLATIO: Oral stimulation of a penis.

FITNESS: An organism's ability to thrive in an environment, generally considered to be a combination of its capacities to survive and to reproduce.

GENDER: For humans, the division of people into categories based on social and cultural roles and behavior. For animals, this book takes on biologist Joan Roughgarden's definition of gender as "how an organism presents and carries out a sexual role."

GENETIC MONOGAMY: Sexual exclusivity between two members of the same species. (related: social monogamy)

GENOTYPE: An organism's genetic composition, including both the sequences of genetic code that are expressed and those that aren't coded into proteins. (related: phenotype)

GONOCHORISTIC: Describes animals in which most individuals fall into male or female categories, and do not change sex over their lifetimes.

GROUP SELECTION: A form of natural selection in which traits are favored that improve a group's fitness, even if they don't necessarily favor individual fitness.

HERMAPHRODITIC: Describes creatures that have the capacity to possess male and female sexual organs, whether at the same time (**simultaneous hermaphrodite**) or at different times in their life span (**sequential hermaphrodite**). Note: though "hermaphrodite" is still widely used to refer to nonhumans, it is considered offensive for humans, for whom "intersex" is the more commonly used term.

HETEROSEXUAL: Relating to desire for the opposite gender or sex.

HOMOSEXUAL: Relating to desire for one's own gender or sex.

INTERSEX: See page 25 ("What Queer Means").

INVERTEBRATE: An animal without a backbone.

LEK: A breeding-season arena in which males display to impress other animals of the same species.

MENTALISTIC: Relating to the mind, and decisions made from an individual's mental processes.

MICROVILLI: Microscopic protrusions from a cell's membrane. Used by an egg to help maneuver a sperm.

MODALITY: One way of expressing something.

MONOMORPHIC: Displaying in only one form. (In sexually monomorphic species, males and females have no differences in outward appearance.)

NATURAL SELECTION: The process, popularized by Charles Darwin, through which organisms that are best suited to their environments thrive and pass more of their genetic code to their descendants, altering a species over time.

NONBINARY: Relating to someone who does not identify as a man or woman, within the traditional gender binary. Also sometimes called "enby" (*n+b*). Can also refer to thinking that doesn't simplify an issue into two sides.

OXYTOCIN: A hormone released during childbirth and during periods of bonding. Sometimes called the "love hormone." It, or some version of it, is thought to exist in all vertebrates and many invertebrates.

PANSEXUAL: Relating to desire for others not limited by sex or gender expression.

PARASITISM: Relying on another organism for survival or for the raising of one's offspring.

PARASITOID: An insect whose larva are parasites that eventually kill their hosts.

PARTHENOGENETIC: Producing offspring without mating, through a so-called virgin birth.

PATRIARCHAL: Related to a society governed or controlled by males.

PHENOTYPE: The physical expression of genes (e.g., eye color, height). (related: genotype)

PHEROMONE: A chemical released by an organism that alters the behavior of others of their own species.

PHYLOGENETIC CONVERGENCE: Independent evolution of similar features in species that are separated by time or distance.

POLYAMORY: Having more than one romantic or sexual relationship at a time.

PRIMATE: A member of the order of life Primates, which includes monkeys, apes, lemurs, lorises, tarsiers, and galagos. Oh—and also humans.

PRIMATOLOGY: The study of monkeys and apes, conventionally excluding humans. (related: anthropology, anthropocentrism)

PROTANDRY: Beginning life as male before changing to female. (related: protogyny)

PROTOGYNY: Beginning life as female before changing to male. (related: protandry)

QUEER: See page 25 ("What Queer Means").

SAME-SEX SEXUAL BEHAVIOR: See page 25 ("What Queer Means").

SENTIENCE: The ability to experience emotions, like pleasure and pain.

SEX: Either (a) the division of a species by reproductive function ("his sex was assigned as male") or (b) physical expression of instinct or attraction drawing organisms together ("the two beetles had sex").

SEX-SEGREGATED: Refers to animal societies in which males and females live most of their existences apart from one another.

SEXUAL ORIENTATION: A being's identity in relation to the sex(es) or gender(s) they are attracted to.

SEXUAL SELECTION: Natural selection in which mate selection is the driver of a species' change over time.

SEXUALITY: Either a being's potential for sexual feelings, or their relation to the gender or genders to which they're attracted.

SOCIAL MONOGAMY: Long-term cohabitation by two members of the same species. (related: genetic monogamy)

SODOMY: Conventionally describes anal sex, but can technically refer to any nonprocreative sex (e.g., oral sex, manual stimulation). Almost always negative in connotation.

SUPERNORMAL: Describes a nest with more eggs than is typical for a given species.

TRANSGENDER: Relating to someone whose personal identity does not correspond with their sex assigned at birth. (related: cisgender)

TWO-SPIRIT: A term used by some Indigenous North Americans to refer to people who fill a role that in some way varies from the male-female binary.

ZOOLOGY: The scientific study of animals.

NOTES

INTRODUCTION: THE IMMORALITY OF PENGUINS

1: "it has Europe's oldest exhibit of them, dating back to 1913": Edinburgh Zoo, "Our History," accessed August 17, 2021, www.edinburghzoo.org.uk/our-history/.

1: "was even knighted": Edinburgh Zoo, "Sir Nils Olav," accessed August 17, 2021, www.edinburghzoo.org.uk/animals-and-attractions/sir-nils-olav/.

1: "The trouble started soon after": Bagemihl, *Biological Exuberance*, 95.

2: "The 1920s public had to come to terms . . .": Gillespie, *King Penguins*, 96–120 (Bertha and Caroline on p. 98).

2: "Levick discovered 'depraved' behavior in wild Adélies": Russell, "Dr. George Murray Levick," 3.

2: "it emerged that a 'gay' couple of penguins stole an egg": Wong, "Gay male penguins steal."

3: "in over 1,500 animal species": Kamath et al., "Why Is Same-Sex Sexual Behavior So Common in Animals?"

3: "studies setting out to catalog homosexual behavior in the animal world are still rare"; "There are thousands of examples of SSB [same-sex sexual behavior] in animals, he said, yet most of these observations occurred by chance and scientists rarely if ever actively study how often these behaviors occur compared with different-sex sexual behaviors": Max Lambert, indirectly quoted in Dennehy, "Should Scientists Change How They View (and Study) Same Sex Behavior in Animals?"

3: "a freshman in Wyoming, Matthew Shepard": Jude Sheerin, "Matthew Shepard: The murder that changed America," BBC News, October 26, 2018, www.bbc.com/news/world-us -canada-45968606.

4: "That was only the most famous case of the hundreds of people killed each year for being queer": Wareham, "Murdered, Suffocated and Burned Alive."

4: "exhaustive, meticulously researched *Biological Exuberance*"; "a scholarly, exhaustive, and utterly convincing refutation of the notion that human homosexuality is an aberration in nature." *Kirkus Reviews,* "Biological Exuberance," November 1, 1998, www.kirkusreviews .com/book-reviews/bruce-bagemihl/biological-exuberance/; "this book presents to the lay reader and specialist alike an exhaustively argued case that animals have multiple shades of sexual orientation." *Publishers Weekly,* "Biological Exuberance," accessed August 17, 2021, www.publishersweekly.com/978-0-312-19239-6.

5: "In the past, scientists would avoid publishing on queer animal behavior because they found it shameful"; "Many records of [same-sex sexual behavior] come from incidental observations, and far more may have gone unreported because researchers either did not recognize behaviors or considered them shameful, unimportant or simply irrelevant to the studies they were conducting": Monk et al., "An Alternative Hypothesis," 1628.

5: "George Murray Levick": Russell, "Dr. George Murray Levick," 4.

5: "a US government document removed all references to homosexual behavior": Balcomb et al., "Killer Whale," 1979:23; Balcomb et al., "Observations of Killer Whales," report no. MMC-78/13 to US Marine Mammal Commission, NTIS# PB80-224728. Cited in Bagemihl, *Biological Exuberance*, 104.

6: "Maybe penguins themselves couldn't recognize sex differences, they argued"; (The typical penguin is) "unaware of sex differences and does not differentiate between males and females even in mating": Roberts, "The Breeding Behavior of Penguins," 212–3.

6: "a definitive study of wild king penguins": Pincemy et al., "Homosexual Mating Displays in Penguins," 1210.

7: "homosexual males often have sisters who are more fertile than other women": Futuyma, *Evolution*, 595.

7: "fluid sexuality increases reproduction chances across a population"; "Breeding homosexual animals might have an even higher fertility rate than breeding heterosexual animals because homosexually bonded friendships might access more resources than those available to exclusively heterosexual animals": Roughgarden, *Evolution's Rainbow*, 156.

8: "without having an evolutionary impact"; "A focus on adaptation can lead to the interpretation that extant traits are the most recent manifestation of evolutionary change under strong natural selection, rather than emergent properties borne of weak or absent selection, fluctuating selective pressures and biological constraints." Monk et al., "An Alternative Hypothesis," 1627.

INTERLUDE: WHO I AM

10: "eight of the top ten banned books the year I write this": Flood, "LGBTQ children's books."

10: "horrific conditions": ASPCA, "Animals on Factory Farms."

11: "The number of aquatic creatures killed by industrial fishing": Based on numbers from the United Nations Food & Agriculture Organization as reported by Fishcount.org.uk, "Fish Count Estimates," 2019, Accessed February 7, 2022. fishcount.org.uk/fish-count-estimates-2#farmedestimate.

12: "large ocean fish populations": *National Geographic,* "Overfishing."

CHAPTER 1: DOODLEBUGS

14: Bagemihl epigraph: *Biological Exuberance,* 84.

14: "August Kelch had a suspicion": Kelch, "Bastardbegattung," 737.

15: "'stronger of the two had forced itself on the smaller and weaker one'": Kelch, "Bastardbe-gattung," 737–38, translated in Brooks, "All Too Human," 148. I'm indebted to Brooks's article for compiling this history of European research into doodlebug same-sex sexual behavior.

16: "it has been tolerated or embraced in 64 percent of them, in fact, as noted by a recent study": Kirkpatrick, "The Evolution of Human Homosexual Behavior," 385.

16: Discussion of rise of intolerance in thirteenth century: Boswell, *Christianity, Social Tolerance, and Homosexuality*, 59, 293.

17: Aquinas and Corbeil discussion: Joyce Salisbury, *The Beast Within*, 65.

17: "'a curious physical form of penetrated parties'": This quote is how Brooks characterized the language of this untranslated article, in "All Too Human," 148. The title of Doebner's 1850 essay, "ueber scheinbar abnorme antennenform bei *Melolontha vulgaris*," literally translates to "on apparently abnormal antenna shape in *Melolontha vulgaris*."

17: "'fraglichen Weibchen'": Brooks, "All Too Human," 148.

18: Illustration: Gadeau de Kerville, H., "Perversion sexuelle chez des Coléoptères mâles." *Bulletin de la sociéte entomologique de France* 4: 85. (Illustration originally presented without a caption, signed by A. L. Clement, and reprinted in Brooks, 153.)

18: "Sodomy criminalization": Levy, Michael, "Gay rights movement." Encyclopedia Britannica, June 15, 2020. www.britannica.com/topic/gay-rights-movement.

18: "the 'unnaturalness' of their act was a crucial component of their sentencing": Despret, "For Queer," in *What Would Animals Say*, 134–35.

18: "citing in their decision the waves of research": American Psychological Association, American Psychiatric Association, National Association of Social Workers, Texas Chapter of the National Association of Social Workers, "Brief for Amici Curiae in Support of Petitioners in the case of *John Geddes Lawrence and Tyron Garner v. State of Texas*," January 2003. accessed February 7, 2022, https://www.americanbar.org/content/dam/aba/administrative/amicus/lawrence.pdf.

19: Hyenas and partridges: Salisbury, *The Beast Within*, 65.

19: "the Duke of Nevers brought thousands of goats": Dekkers, *Dearest Pet*, 18.

19: "homosexual activity is common in elephants": Bagemihl, *Biological Exuberance*, 427–30.

19: "'as they lacked lust . . .'": Salisbury, *The Beast Within*, 66.

20: Articles containing "condemning words": Bagemihl, *Biological Exuberance*, 89.

21: "'The interesting philosophical considerations which arise from such abnormal phenomena, I leave to the reader himself to address'": Quoted in Brooks, "All Too Human," 150.

21: "'man-manly mating between insects'": Quoted in Brooks, "All Too Human," 152.

21: "'pédérastie par gout'": Quoted in Brooks, "All Too Human," 153. Note that, though the modern use of *pederasty* indicates sexual activity between a man and a boy, Gadeau de Kerville was using it in the archaic form, which referred to generalized male homosexual behavior.

22: "'congenital sexual inversion seems to belong exclusively to man'": Charles Samson Féré, *The sexual instinct: its evolution and dissolution* (translated by H. Blanchamp). London: University Press, 1900, 92.

22: "same-sex behavior 'in arthropods is predominantly based on mistaken identification'": Scharf, "Same-Sex Behavior in Insects and Arachnids," 1719.

22: "Another group of scientists independently supported this theory": Engel et al., "Acceptance Threshold Theory," 2.

24: James Weinrich quote: Quoted in Sommer, *Homosexual Behaviour in Animals*, 368.

INTERLUDE: WHAT QUEER MEANS

27: "most plants are hermaphrodites . . .": Jarne and Auld, "Animals Mix It Up," 1816.

28: "The definition of sex that some biologists use": Roughgarden, *Evolution's Rainbow*, 23.

28: "'how an organism presents and carries out a sexual role'": Roughgarden, *Evolution's Rainbow*, 28.

28: "such as in chickens!": Roughgarden, *Evolution's Rainbow*, 27.

CHAPTER 2: BONOBOS

34: Introducing honey to a group of chimps: De Waal, *Bonobo*, 76.

35: "'The chimpanzee resolves sexual issues with power; the bonobo resolves power issues with sex'": De Waal, *Bonobo*, 32.

35: "as much as eight times a day": De Waal, *"Bonobo Sex and Society."*

36: "primatologists call it the 'bonobo handshake'": Woods, *Bonobo Handshake*, 208;

36: "young bonobos will sometimes mount their older and higher ranking troopmates": De Waal, *Bonobo*, 103.

36: "Bonobos will also have sex face-to-face": De Waal, *Bonobo*, 101.

37: "homosexual encounters among bonobos are actually *more* common than heterosexual ones": Clay and de Waal, "Sex and Strife," 314.

37: "logging all the sexual activity of the bonobos": Hohmann and Fruth, "Use and Function of Genital Contacts," 107–120.

38: "'If you're looking for homosexual sex in vast quantities, forget humans, it's bonobos you want'": Cited in Vines, "Queer Creatures," 35.

39: Sigmund Freud argument re: bisexuality: as summarized in Kirkpatrick, "The Evolution of Human Homosexual Behavior," 397.

CHAPTER 3: FRUIT FLIES

48: "What 'causes' homosexuality is an issue of importance only to societies which regard gay people as bizarre or anomalous": Boswell, *Christianity, Social Tolerance, and Homosexuality*, 48.

48: Homosexuality a disorder in the *DSM*: Jack Dresher, "Out of DSM," 565.

48: Quotes from respected psychotherapists and criminologists: Quoted in Richard Horton, "Is Homosexuality Inherited?," *New York Review of Books*.

49: 23andMe discussion: Lambert, "No 'Gay Gene,'" 3.

49: Dan Quayle on homosexuality as "a wrong choice": Karen DeWitt, "The 1992 Campaign: The Vice President; Quayle Contends Homosexuality Is a Matter of Choice, Not Biology," September 14, 1992, www.nytimes.com/1992/09/14/us/1992-campaign-vice-president-quayle-contends-homosexuality-matter-choice-not.html.

50: Treatment of queer people in Nazi Germany: Holocaust Memorial Day Trust, "Gay People," accessed August 17, 2021, www.hmd.org.uk/learn-about-the-holocaust-and-genocides/nazi-persecution/gay-people/.

50: "'While homosexuals are more likely to have been effeminate as boys'": Dennis Werner, "The Evolution of Male Homosexuality and Its Implications for Human Psychological and Cultural Variations," in *Homosexual Behavior in Animals*, ed. Sommer and Vasey, 328.

51: "'While many self-identified homosexuals recall a gender-atypical childhood'": Kirkpatrick, "Evolution of Human Homosexual Behavior," 390.

51: Reasons fruit flies are the most studied multicellular organisms: Dutchen, "Why the Fly?"

51: "75 percent of the genes that cause disease in humans have equivalents in fruit flies": Dutchen, "Why the Fly?"

52: "led the Associated Press to report": Mills, "Researchers Induce Homosexual Behavior in Male Fruit Flies."

52: "using estrogen inhibitors": Adkins-Regan, "Development of Sexual Partner Preference."

52: "making lesions on the brains of male ferrets": Paredes and Baum, "Altered Sexual Partner Preference."

53: "'how simplistic it seems to equate genital licking in Drosophila with complex individual and social homosexual behavior in humans.'": Horton, "Is Homosexuality Inherited?," 1.

54: Paragraph beginning "Research into the genetics of human sexuality": Saravi, "The Elusive Search for a 'Gay Gene,'" 462.

55: "utterly contradictory information": Saravi, "The Elusive Search for a 'Gay Gene,'" 463.

56: "'50 to 60 percent of sexual orientation might be genetic'": Kristof, "Gay at Birth?"

56: "'On the one hand, we are pleased . . .'": quoted in Saravi, "The Elusive Search for a 'Gay Gene,'" 467.

57: "'The question is . . .'": Horton, "Is Homosexuality Inherited?," 6.

57: "'there is no gay gene,'" Quoted in Lambert, "No 'Gay Gene,'" 2.

CHAPTER 4: BOTTLENOSE DOLPHINS

65: "Frisky young dolphin males have sexual contact an average of 2.38 times an hour . . . and the majority of that is with other males": Janet Mann, "Establishing Trust," 122.

65: "'Grindr has announced a new gay cruising app for dolphins'": *Capital Xtra* (Ottawa), 5.

66: Paragraph beginning "We've known for decades": Mann, "Establishing Trust," 108.

66: "'the most complex non-human society on the planet'": Quoted in Krista Carothers, "Why Dolphins Are Some of the Smartest Creatures on the Planet," *Reader's Digest*, January 22, 2020, rd.com/list/dolphins-smartest-creatures/.

67: "With few exceptions, these males all have sex with females, too": Mann, "Establishing Trust," 126–27.

67: "it's hard to tell exactly who's mounting whom": "For example, when bottle-nosed dolphins constantly roll and shift as they manipulate each other's genital area with their beaks, fins and genitalia, no individual can be unambiguously labeled mounter or mountee." Sommer and Vasey, "Introduction," *Homosexual Behaviour in Animals,* 22.

67: "'the owner of the erection was not identified'" through end of paragraph: Mann, "Establishing Trust," 112.

67: Art caption, "We female dolphins have evolved these labyrinthine vaginas in response": Gabbatiss, "Female dolphins have weaponised."

68: "for many whale species, even familiar ones like blues and humpbacks, *no* sex of any sort has ever been observed": Clapham, "The Social and Reproductive Biology," 37.

68: "The only reason we know about same-sex sexual behavior in dolphins and killer whales": Smolker, Richards, Connor, and Pepper, "Sex Differences in Patterns," 39.

68: "they both also show significant amounts of same-sex sexual activity": Bagemihl, *Biological Exuberance*, 349.

68: "'Homosexuality' as a term is actually a fairly modern invention": Oxford English Dictionary, s.v. "homosexual, adj. and n."

70: "One significant historical study of all known human societies"; "In Ford and Beach's (1951) world sample, homosexual behavior is normative in 64% of the societies with available data (n=76) at least for certain classes of individuals": Kirkpatrick, "The Evolution of Human Homosexual Behavior," 385.

71: "Especially substantial cases numbers of homosexual relationships are found in": Kirkpatrick, "The Evolution of Human Homosexual Behavior," 394.

71: "In fact, people looked at men who *didn't* enjoy sex with other men as suspiciously effeminate": Boswell, *Christianity, Social Tolerance, and Homosexuality*, 24–25.

71: "Greek heroes like Achilles and Heracles had same-sex exploits": Pickett, *The Stanford Encyclopedia of Philosophy*.

71: "'they who . . . hang about men and embrace them, and they are themselves the best of boys and youths, because they have the most manly nature'": Plato, *The Symposium*, 231.

71: "'Homer's Nestor was not well skilled'": Plutarch, *Select Lives*, 68.

72: "'in his adolescence he drew away the husbands from their wives, and as a young man the wives from their husbands'": Quoted in Pickett, *The Stanford Encyclopedia of Philosophy*.

72: "These romantic relationships between men weren't just about sex. They also produced advantageous bonds": As one anthropologist summarized it, in the sort of language often reserved for animal behavior, "homosexual behavior comes from individual selection for reciprocal altruism." Kirkpatrick, "The Evolution of Human Homosexual Behavior," 385.

72: "When men came together from wealthy families, it was the result of lengthy courtship and parental discussions to make sure that this male sexual union was noble love, not just sex"; "In this relationship there was courtship ritual, involving gifts (such as a rooster), and other norms. The erastes had to show that he had nobler interests in the boy, rather than a purely sexual concern. The boy was not to submit too easily, and if pursued by more than one man, was to show discretion and pick the more noble one." *Pickett, The Stanford Encyclopedia of Philosophy*.

73: "There is evidence that the Spartans also supported sexual relationships between women, with a similar mentor-trainee dynamic": Dover, *Greek Homosexuality*, 173.

73: "the 'olisbo,' a leather dildo": Roughgarden, *Evolution's Rainbow*, 368.

CHAPTER 5: JAPANESE MACAQUES

78: "'Conditions in the vagina are very inhospitable . . .'": Keeton, *Biological Sciences,* 394.

79: "All along, there have been microvilli on the exterior of the egg": Schatten and Schatten, "The Energetic Egg," 31.

79–80: "'Ever since the invention of the light microscope . . .'": Schatten and Schatten, "The Energetic Egg," 34.

81: Rhesus macaques example: Ellen Kapsalis and Rodney L. Johnson, "Getting to Know You: Female-Female Consortships in Free-Ranging Rhesus Monkeys," chapter 9 in *Homosexual Behaviour in Animals,* 220–237.

81: "This has led primatologists to caution that there might not be a blanket homosexual behavior common to macaques, but rather plural homosexual behaviors": Vasey, "The pursuit of pleasure . . . Japanese Macaques," chapter 8 in *Homosexual Behaviour in Animals,* 192.

82: "'exhibit a reddening of the face and perineum that is associated with increased receptivity and proceptivity'": Vasey, "The pursuit of pleasure," 194.

82: "'it's a social interaction that has nothing to do with sexual pleasure'": Craig Packer from the Lion Center in Minnesota, quoted in Adriaens, "In Defence of Animal Homosexuality," 14.

82: "Paul Vasey and his laboratory set out to examine the various possible motives": Vasey, "The pursuit of pleasure," 208–13.

83: "'subordinate consort partners were more likely to perform same-sex sexual solicitations and mounts before an aggressive interaction than after'": Vasey, "The pursuit of pleasure," 212.

83: "'Despite over 40 years of intensive research on this species, there is not a single study demonstrating any adaptive value for female-female sexual behaviour in Japanese macaques'": Vasey, "The pursuit of pleasure," 213.

84: "'When a male Giraffe sniffs'": Bagemihl, *Biological Exuberance*, 117. Bagemihl also notes that "simple genital nuzzling of a female Vicuña [a relative of the llama] by a male—taking place outside of the breeding season, and without any mounting or copulation to accompany it—is classified as sexual behavior, while actual same-sex mounting in the same species is considered nonsexual or 'play' behavior," 117.

85: "Cardi B's WAP": Jordan Moreau, "Cardi B Slams U.S. Representative for Debating 'WAP' Performance Over Police Brutality," *Variety*, April 22, 2021, variety.com/2021/music/news /cardi-b-wap-grammys-performance-1234958146/.

85: Sigmund Freud quotes: *New Introductory Lectures,* 167.

86: Linda Wolfe quote: Vines, "Queer Creatures," 34.

CHAPTER 6: DEER

93: "'the musculature becomes limp . . .'": Lorenz, *Here I Am—Where Are You?*, 251.

93–94: "bisexuality came earlier in the history of life than homo- or heterosexuality"; "Indeed, when we observe a particular trait [same-sex sexual behavior existing alongside different-sex sexual behavior] so prevalent within a clade, a reasonable hypothesis to explain such an evolutionary pattern is that the trait likely arose near the clade's origins.": Monk et al., "An Alternative Hypothesis," 1622.

95: "They skip the bachelor herds and the groups of mothers, and instead form their own troops of three to seven velvet-horns": Thomas, Robinson, and Marburger, "Social Behavior in a White-Tailed Deer Herd," 317.

96: "'excellent body fat deposits'": Bagemihl, *Biological Exuberance*, 380.

96: "Since the velvet-horns don't mate, they don't produce their own offspring, but if they come across an orphaned fawn, they will incorporate them into their group to rear": Thomas, Robinson, and Marburger, "Social Behavior in a White-Tailed Deer Herd," 317.

96–97: Discussion of mule deer and cactus bucks: Thomas, Robinson, and Marburger, "Social Behavior in a White-Tailed Deer Herd," 314.

96: "Similarly nonreproductive intersex animals": Roughgarden, *Evolution's Rainbow,* 37.

96: Paragraph beginning "There is another sort of intersexuality": Roughgarden, *Evolution's Rainbow,* 78.

98: "Various dolphin and whale species have intersex individuals that have genitalia of both sexes": Roughgarden, *Evolution's Rainbow,* 41.

98: "Males of many bird species undergo": Slagsvold and Sætre, "Evolution of Plumage Color," 915.

98: "Some garter snake males": Shine, Langkilde, and Mason, "Confusion within 'Mating Balls.'" The phenomenon is also described in Bailey and Zuk, "Same-Sex Sexual Behavior and Evolution," when they note that garter snakes will mimic females "in size or pheromone attributes, and are courted by other males when females are absent. However, male-male courtship is not likely a result of mistaken sex recognition; attractive male courtship might allow solitary males to thermoregulate and protect themselves," 2.

98: "there are many animals that do not ever reproduce": Bagemihl, *Biological Exuberance,* 196.

98: "whiptail lizards": Crews, "Courtship in Unisexual Lizards."

CHAPTER 7: WRASSE FISH

107: Paragraph beginning "She's a bluestreak cleaner wrasse": Robertson, "Social Control of Sex Reversal in a Coral-Reef Fish."

107: Paragraph beginning "This isn't unique to the bluestreak cleaner wrasse": Helfman, *Diversity of Fishes,* 458.

107: Clown fish discussion: Moyer and Nakazono, "Protandrous Hermaphroditism in Six Species," 103–5. Note that if a fish is an external fertilizer and there is a lot of competing sperm floating around its environment (like for fish that live in seagrass beds), sometimes females will not transition even after the dominant male dies—it's more advantageous to remain female than to enter the sperm competition. See Muñoz and Warner, "A New Version of the Size-Advantage Hypothesis."

108: "Some species of frogs and lizards, for example, change sex as needed within their local groups": Lambert et al., "Molecular Evidence for Sex Reversal."

109: "It's advantageous for your average wrasse female": Robertson, "Social Control of Sex Reversal in a Coral-Reef Fish," 1009.

109–110: Flatworm discussion: Bondar, *Wild Sex*, 111.

110: "Other fish are parthenogenetic": Helfman, *Diversity of Fishes*, 460.

110: "Some parrotfish are born male, and some are born female": This discussion of parrotfish is drawn from Robertson and Warner, "Sexual Patterns in the Labroid Fishes"; and R. R. Warner and I. F. Downs, "Comparative Life Histories: Growth versus Reproduction in Normal Males and Sex-Changing Hermaphrodites in the Striped Parrotfish," *Proceedings of the Third International Symposium on Coral Reefs* 1 (Biology) (1977): 275–82. Cited in Bagemihl, *Biological Exuberance*, 40.

112: "Frogs and lizards will change sex": Lambert et al., "Molecular Evidence for Sex Reversal in Wild Populations of Green Frogs."

112: "having male and female genitalia is the standard way of life for the majority of plants": Roughgarden, *Evolution's Rainbow*, 27.

112: Sea snails discussion: "When given a choice of mates, small *C. fornicata* males paired more often with females than with large males, although some males always chose other males as partners." Ambrogio and Pechenik, "When Is a Male Not a Male?," 1782.

113: "'the importance of active choice in the behavior of species that are generally considered to possess little agency over their reproductive fitness'": Ambrogio and Pechenik, "When Is a Male Not a Male?," 1785.

CHAPTER 8: ALBATROSS

122: "with a wingspan upward of six and a half feet": The Cornell Lab of Ornithology, "Laysan Albatross Identification."

122: "Though they nest on the Hawaiian Islands, Laysan albatrosses fly as far as California or Japan to feed": The Cornell Lab of Ornithology, "Laysan Albatross Overview."

123: "as researcher Lindsay Young observed, the female couples 'behave just like male-female pairs . . . if a male comes up to one female in the pair, the second female gets really possessive'": Choi, "Female Albatrosses Shack Up."

123–24: Paragraph beginning "Sometimes only one female gets inseminated": Young and VanderWerf, "Adaptive Value of Same-Sex Pairing in Laysan Albatross," 3.

124: "This has led some scientists to argue that these two otherwise single parents are 'making the best of a bad job' in response to a shortage of males": Young and VanderWerf, "Adaptive Value of Same-Sex Pairing in Laysan Albatross," 4.

124: Paul Vasey quotes: Quoted in Vines, "Queer Creatures," 35.

125–26: "'further study of homosexually paired female birds may help clarify what, if anything, males are good for—in an evolutionary sense, of course'": Diamond, "Goslings of Gay Geese," 101. He goes on to note: "These observations raise the perennial question of why males exist at all at a sex ratio near 1.0. After a male gull has contributed semen, he appears to play almost no role that a female cannot play equally well . . . if long-term reproductive success per egg is at least 50 per cent of normal, homosexual pairs would still have a higher reproductive output per individual than do heterosexual species."

126: "Researcher Lindsay Young argues that female-female nesting is found in 'not just albatrosses, but other seabirds as well. This may be a lot more common than we realized, so the race is on to find out'": Choi, "Female Albatrosses."

126: "About 12 percent of the nests in one population of roseate terns": Vines, "Queer Creatures," 35.

126: "Similar percentages of female-female nesting are found in gulls and jackdaws. In these species, females will make a joint nest, a large structure with separate spots for each bird's eggs. In Canada geese and mute swans, the female pairs will construct separate but adjacent nests": Bagemihl, *Biological Exuberance*, 25.

127: "Male mute swans may bond for life just like female pairs do, even though their nests are empty. Same for black-crowned night herons and great cormorants": Bagemihl, *Biological Exuberance*, 25.

127: All three examples in paragraph beginning "Altruism springs up": Okasha, *The Stanford Encyclopedia of Philosophy*.

128: "Pairs of male cheetahs will parent lost cubs, and female pairs of northern elephant seals adopt orphaned pups": Bagemihl, *Biological Exuberance*, 24.

129: Quote beginning "sometimes two female animals": Bagemihl, *Biological Exuberance*, 23.

129: "In still other species, such as squirrel monkeys and greater rheas": Bagemihl, *Biological Exuberance*, 23–24.

CHAPTER 9: BULLS

132: All Simon Amor quotes: Nichols, "What's It Like Collecting."

133: "When each bull is ejaculated two to three times a week, and two or three times each ejaculation day, they can start resisting": Smith, "Life as a Bull Stud."

133: "Some recent sales pamphlets": Kathryn Gillespie, "Sexualized Violence and the Gendered Commodification," 1328.

133: "an Angus bull broke records by selling for $1.5 million"; Art reference to electroejaculation: Smith, "Life as a Bull Stud."

134: "In fact, females will mount other females so often that farmers will use that to identify when they're in heat"; "First off, if a bull has gotten used to steers, he'll begin to favor them entirely over female cows": Denniston, "Ambisexuality in Animals," in *Homosexual Behavior: A Modern Reappraisal*, 34.

135: Quote beginning with "Male-male mounting": Hilde Vervaecke and Catherine Roden, "Going with the herd," chapter 5 in Sommer and Vasey, *Homosexual Behaviour in Animals*, 132.

135: Quote beginning with "Cattle in mixed-sex herds": Monk et al., "An Alternative hypothesis," 1625. (Referencing Vasey, "Same-Sex Sexual Partner Preference," 141–79.)

135–36: "There's the visual difference, with udders and horns and penises all clearly marking who's who, and cattle also use scent to distinguish individuals and determine their sex": G. Archunan et al., "Cattle Pheromones," chapter 16 in *Neurobiology of Chemical Communication*.

136: "It could just be a harmless by-product of evolution's building a stronger and stronger sex drive in cattle in general"; "Many instances of homosexual mounting . . . could represent functionless by-products of males' low threshold for sexual excitement—a tendency that is, on balance, adaptive"; "Animal homosexual behaviour is not always enacted to mediate adaptive social or reproductive functions, but it may exist simply for sexual gratification. Selection against the behaviour does not occur because it does not interfere with reproduction." Sommer and Vasey, "Introduction," *Homosexual Behaviour in Animals*, 33.

136: "Often these observations were couched in judgmental language": Quotes in Bagemihl, *Biological Exuberance*, 88–9.

137: "Nearly 8 percent of them fall into this category": LeVay, *Gay, Straight, and the Reason Why*, 38.

137: "over a three-year period the number varied anywhere between 15 and 30 percent": Cited in Terry, "'Unnatural Acts' in Nature," 179.

137: "only ending in anal penetration rather than vaginal": LeVay, *Gay, Straight, and the Reason Why*, 38.

137: Paragraph beginning "The existence of exclusively homosexual sheep": "Is Your Ram a Dud or a Stud?," as quoted in Roughgarden, *Evolution's Rainbow*, 139.

138: "the rams lived in essentially a homosexual society": Valerius Geist quoted in Vines, "Queer Creatures," 34.

138: Details in the three paragraphs beginning with "In the wild, sheep live": Bagemihl, *Biological Exuberance*, 406–7.

138: Two paragraphs starting "This public outing of the habits of cows": Anderson and Binstein, "Suppressing Sex Studies."

139: "The rodeo, our Americanized version of the bullfighting traditions of Europe that prize the aggressive virility of the bull and matador above all else": While we're on the topic of the rodeo—it's brutal on the animals involved, which are exempt from the protections of the federal Animal Welfare Act. The Humane Society of the United States officially "opposes rodeos as they are commonly organized, since they typically cause torment and stress to animals, expose them to pain, injury or even death and encourage an insensitivity to and acceptance of the inhumane treatment of animals in the name of sport." Humane Society of the United States, "Our Policies," accessed August 18, 2021, www.humanesociety.org/our-policies.

CHAPTER 10: DUCKS AND GEESE

146: "three-ways most likely have a long-standing role in the evolutionary history of the wolf spider": Persons, "Field Observations of Simultaneous Double Mating."

151–52: "This leads to high levels of mortality in nesting birds": Sanders, "Causes of Mortality at Nests of Ground-Nesting Birds."

152: "Gulls, especially, will regularly go smash up the unattended eggs of other gulls": Diamond, "Goslings of Gay Geese."

152: "more than 90 percent of bird species are *socially* monogamous, meaning the birds choose one partner, only finding another if the first dies or disappears, but *genetic* monogamy occurs in only 25 percent of bird species": Griffith, Owens, and Thuman, "Extra Pair Paternity in Birds," 1.

152: "In the geese, upward of 10 percent of their nests are cared for by thruples instead of couples": Weiß, "Alternative Social and Reproductive Strategies," 94.

153: Philippe Carruette quote: Menendez, dir., "Animal Homosexuality," *Animals Like Us*.

153: "only about 20 percent of heterosexual pairs manage to raise young to fledging": Weiß, "Alternative Social and Reproductive Strategies," 93.

153: "the rates are higher for these three-goose nests": Menendez, dir., "Animal Homosexuality," *Animals Like Us*.

153: "The triumph ceremony is important to greylag society": Lorenz, *The Triumph Ceremony*."

154: Paragraph beginning "Sometimes a female will return to the same male couple": Menendez, dir., "Animal Homosexuality," *Animals Like Us*.

154: "It's not just that these males occasionally had sex with males; they could actually be said to have a homosexual orientation, meaning an exclusive interest in courting and bonding with other males": Weiß, "Alternative Social and Reproductive Strategies," 90.

154: "there are many other bird species that do, like the pukeko, Eurasian oystercatcher, gulls, and terns": Bagemihl, *Biological Exuberance*, *s.v.* individual animal entries.

154–55: "some female mallard ducks will perform what's known as the 'pumping' display, a prelude to mating, and then will copulate with another female": Bagemihl, *Biological Exuberance*, 492.

155: "Konrad Lorenz recounts an amusing story about a parrot breeder": Lorenz, *Here I Am— Where Are You?*, 231.

156: "When males shack up, they tend to make a lot more noise and ruckus than male-female couples do": "Robert Huber once conducted a quantitative analysis of the behavioral differences between heterosexual pairs and gander pairs. It emerged that each of the males in a gander pair showed vigilance only slightly more often than other ganders did. But the doubling effect resulted in the gander pairs performing this behavior pattern about 2.2 times more frequently than the others, on average." Lorenz, *Here I Am—Where Are You?*, 244–45.

157: "'The difference in mind between man and the higher animals, great as it is, certainly is one of degree and not of kind'": Darwin, *The Descent of Man*, 105.

157: Lorenz quotes in paragraph beginning "Science as we commonly think of it": Lorenz, *Here I Am—Where Are You?*, 258, 262.

Q&A: DYLAN SANBORN

161: "There are 130 different bird species on the record as having same-sex behaviors": MacFarlane et al., "Same-Sex Sexual Behavior in Birds."

CONCLUSION

165: Epigraph: MacDonald, *Vesper Flights*, 257.

165: "In the Koran, humans are similarly on the top of a hierarchy, above other animals and plants"; "According to the Quran, the creation of the cosmos is a greater reality than the creation of humankind (Sura 40:57), but human beings have been privileged to occupy a position even higher than the angels as vicegerents of God . . . Muslims, as well as Jews and Christians, have had to face the intrinsic problems of such a position, historically as well as in contemporary global economic, political, and social life." Denny, "Islam and Ecology."

166: "Jane Goodall was ridiculed in the scientific academy for giving her subjects names like Frodo and Fifi": McKie, "Chimps with Everything."

167: Beans Velocci quote: Velocci, "The Battle over Trans Rights."

168: Robin Wall Kimmerer quotes: Kimmerer, *Braiding Sweetgrass*, 55, 58.

169: Discussion of *two-spirit*: O'Brien, ed., *Encyclopedia of Gender and Society*, 64.

170: "One reason why queer animal behavior is missing from your average high school textbook"; "Many records of SSB [same-sex sexual behavior] come from incidental observations, and far more may have gone unreported because researchers either did not recognize behaviours or considered them shameful, unimportant or simply irrelevant to the studies they were conducting." Monk et al., "An Alternative Hypothesis,"1628.

171: Linda Wolfe quotes: Quoted in Vines, "Queer Creatures," 33–34.

171: "1,500 and growing": Monk et al., "An Alternative Hypothesis,"1622.

171: "the authors' methodology was to approach researchers who had preexisting study sites and data sets": Sommer and Vasey, "Introduction" from *Homosexual Behaviour,* 8; Vines, "Queer Creatures," 33.

173: "bisexuality as the essential norm throughout the tree of life, not heterosexuality—incurs little cost in a species' fitness"; "Further, we suggest that selection would only act against SSB [same-sex sexual behaviour] in ecological or social contexts where its costs become prohibitive. Absent such costs in particular lineages, SSB may be retained, because reproductive fitness is likely often maximized at intermediate mixtures of sexual behaviours that balance the costs of specially targeting fertilization-compatible mates with the benefits of an increased number of mating opportunities." Monk et al., "An Alternative Hypothesis," 1623.

173: Paul Vasey quotes: Quoted in Vines, "Queer Creatures," 35.

175: Marlene Zuk quotes: Zuk, "Family Values in Black and White."

SELECTED BIBLIOGRAPHY

Adkins-Regan, Elizabeth. "Development of Sexual Partner Preference in the Zebra Finch: A Socially Monogamous, Pair-Bonding Animal." *Archives of Sexual Behavior* 31, no. 1 (2002): 27–33.

Adriaens, Pieter R. "In Defence of Animal Homosexuality." *Philosophy, Theory, and Practice in Biology* 11, no. 20200929 (2019): 1–19.

"All About Birds. Laysan Albatross." The Cornell Lab of Ornithology. Accessed March 29, 2021. www.allaboutbirds.org/guide/Laysan_Albatross.

Ambrogio, Olivia V., and Jan A. Pechenik. "When Is a Male Not a Male? Sex Recognition and Choice in Two Sex-Changing Species." *Behavioral Ecology and Sociobiology* 62, no. 11 (2008): 1779–86.

Anderson, Jack, and Michael Binstein. "Suppressing Sex Studies." *Washington Post*, June 14, 1992. www.washingtonpost.com/archive/opinions/1992/06/14/suppressing-sex -studies/5c0880c2-b548-4803-beac-2bcb4f60caae.

Animals Like Us. Episode "Animal Homosexuality." Directed by Jessica Menendez, Bertrand Loyer, and Stephane Alexandresco (Saint Thomas Productions, 2005).

"Animals on Factory Farms." ASPCA. Accessed March 29, 2021. www.aspca.org/animal -cruelty/farm-animal-welfare/animals-factory-farms.

Archunan, Govindaraju, Swamynathan Rajanarayanan, and Kandasamy Karthikeyan. "Cattle Pheromones." In *Neurobiology of Chemical Communication*, edited by C. Mucignat-Caretta. Boca Raton, FL: CRC Press/Taylor & Francis (2014): 461–488.

Bagemihl, Bruce. *Biological Exuberance: Animal Homosexuality and Natural Diversity*. New York: St. Martin's Press, 2000.

Bailey, N. W., and M. Zuk. "Same-Sex Sexual Behavior and Evolution." *Trends in Ecology and Evolution* 24, no. 8 (2009): 439–46.

Beldecos, Athena, Sarah Balley, Scott Gilbert, Karen Hicks, Lori Kenschaft, Nancy Niemczyk, Rebecca Rosenberg et al. "The Importance of Feminist Critique for Contemporary Cell Biology." *Hypatia* 3, no. 1 (1988): 61.

Bondar, C. "Homosexuality in Nature." August 14, 2019. carinbondar.com/2019/08/14/homosexuality-in-nature.

Bondar, C. *Wild Sex*. New York: Pegasus Books, 2016.

Boswell, John. *Christianity, Social Tolerance, and Homosexuality: Gay People in Western Europe from the Beginning of the Christian Era to the Fourteenth Century*. Chicago: University of Chicago Press, 1980.

Brooker, Jake S., Christine E. Webb, and Zanna Clay. "Fellatio among Male Sanctuary-Living Chimpanzees During a Period of Social Tension." *Behaviour* 158, no. 1 (2020): 77–87.

Brooks, R. "All Too Human: Responses to Same-Sex Copulation in the Common Cockchafer (*Melolontha melolontha* (L.)), 1834–1900." *Archives of Natural History* 36 (2009): 146–59.

Choi, Charles Q. "Female Albatrosses Shack Up." May 27, 2008. Live Science. www.livescience.com/2576-female-albatrosses-shack.html.

Clapham, Phillip J. "The Social and Reproductive Biology of Humpback Whales: An Ecological Perspective." *Mammal Review* 26, no. 1 (1996): 27–49.

Clay, Zanna, and Frans de Waal. "Sex and Strife: Post-Conflict Sexual Contacts in Bonobos." *Behaviour* 152, nos. 3–4 (2015): 313–34.

Connor, Richard C., and Michael R. Heithaus. "Superalliance of Bottlenose Dolphins." *Nature* 397, no. 6720 (1999): 571–72.

Crews, David. "Courtship in Unisexual Lizards: A Model for Brain Evolution." *Scientific American* 257 (1987): 116–21.

Darwin, Charles. *The Descent of Man, and Selection in Relation to Sex*. Edited by John Tyler Bonner and Robert M. May. Princeton, NJ: Princeton University Press, 2008.

De Waal, Frans. *Bonobo: The Forgotten Ape*. Berkeley: University of California Press, 1997.

De Waal, Frans. "Bonobo Sex and Society." *Scientific American*. June 1, 2006. www .scientificamerican.com/article/bonobo-sex-and-society-2006-06.

Dekkers, Midas. *Dearest Pet: On Bestiality*. London: Verso, 2000.

Demir, Ebru, and Barry J. Dickson. "Fruitless Splicing Specifies Male Courtship Behavior in Drosophila." *Cell* 121, no. 5 (2005): 785–94.

Dennehy, Kevin. "Should Scientists Change How They View (and Study) Same Sex Behavior in Animals?" Yale School of the Environment. November 18, 2019. environment.yale.edu /news/article/yale-paper-challenges-how-scientists-study-same-sex-behavior-in-animals.

Denniston, R. H. "Ambisexuality in Animals." In *Homosexual Behavior: A Modern Reappraisal*, edited by J. Marmor. New York: Basic Books, 1980: 25–40.

Denny, Frederick M. "Islam and Ecology." Environment and Ecology. Accessed March 29, 2021. www.environment-ecology.com/religion-and-ecology/714-islam-and-ecology-a -bestowed-trust-inviting-balanced-stewardship.html.

Despret, Vinciane. *What Would Animals Say If We Asked the Right Questions?* Minneapolis, MN: University of Minnesota Press, 2017.

Diamond, Jared M. "Goslings of Gay Geese." *Nature* 340, no. 6229 (1989): 101.

Dover, Kenneth James. *Greek Homosexuality.* Cambridge: MA: Harvard University Press, 1978.

Drescher, Jack. "Out of DSM: Depathologizing Homosexuality." *Behavioral Sciences* 5, no. 4 (2015): 565–75.

Dutchen, Stephanie. "Why the Fly?" Harvard Medical School. April 2, 2018. hms.harvard.edu/news/why-fly.

Engel, Katharina C., Lisa Männer, Manfred Ayasse, and Sandra Steiger. "Acceptance Threshold Theory Can Explain Occurrence of Homosexual Behaviour." *Biology Letters* 11, no. 1 (2015): 20140603.

"Farm Animal Welfare." ASPCA. Accessed August 18, 2021. www.aspca.org/protecting-farm-animals.

Fausto-Sterling, Anne. "The Five Sexes: Why Male and Female Are Not Enough." *Science* 33 (1993): 20–25.

Feist, Jeremy. "Watersports." *Capital Xtra* (Ottawa), April 12, 2012: 5.

Flood, Alison. "LGBTQ Children's Books Face Record Calls for Bans in US Libraries." *Guardian*, April 21, 2020. www.theguardian.com/books/2020/apr/21/us-libraries-say-lgbtq-children-books-most-calls-for-bans-last-year-alex-gino-george.

Freud, Sigmund. *New Introductory Lectures on Psycho-analysis.* London, United Kingdom: Norton, 1989.

Futuyma, Douglas J. *Evolution.* Edited by Mark Kirkpatrick. Sunderland, MA: Sinauer, 2017.

G., Mady, and J. R. Zuckerberg. *A Quick & Easy Guide to Queer & Trans Identities.* Portland: Limerence Press, 2019.

Gabbatiss, Josh. "Female dolphins have weaponised their vaginas to fend off males." *New Scientist*, October 10, 2017. www.newscientist.com/article/2150052-female-dolphins -have-weaponised-their-vaginas-to-fend-off-males/

Gavrilets, Sergey, and William R. Rice. "Genetic Models of Homosexuality: Generating Testable Predictions." *Proceedings of the Royal Society B: Biological Sciences* 273, no. 1605 (2006): 3031–38.

"Gay People." Holocaust Memorial Day Trust. Accessed March 29, 2021. www.hmd.org .uk/learn-about-the-holocaust-and-genocides/nazi-persecution/gay-people.

Gillespie, Kathryn. "Sexualized Violence and the Gendered Commodification of the Animal Body in Pacific Northwest US Dairy Production." *Gender, Place & Culture* 21, no. 10 (2014): 1321–37.

Gillespie, Thomas Haining. *A Book of King Penguins*. London: H. Jenkins, 1932.

Griffith, Simon, Ian Owens, and Katherine Thuman. "Extra Pair Paternity in Birds: A Review of Interspecific Variation and Adaptive Function." *Molecular Ecology* 11 (2002): 2195–212.

Helfman, Gene S. *The Diversity of Fishes: Biology, Evolution, and Ecology.* Vol. 14. Chichester, UK: Blackwell, 2009.

Hohmann, G., and B. Fruth. "Use and Function of Genital Contacts among Female Bono- bos." *Animal Behaviour* 60, no. 1 (2000): 107–20.

Horton, Richard. "Is Homosexuality Inherited?" *New York Review of Books*, July 13, 1995. www.nybooks.com/articles/1995/07/13/is-homosexuality-inherited.

Huber, R., and M. Martys. "Male-Male Pairs in Greylag Geese (*Anser anser*)." *Journal für Ornithologie* 134, no. 2 (1993): 155–64.

Jarne, P., and J. R. Auld. "Animals Mix It Up Too: The Distribution of Self-Fertilization among Hermaphroditic Animals." *Evolution* 60 (2006): 1816–24.

Kamath, Ambika, Julia Monk, Erin Giglio, Max Lambert, and Caitlin McDonough. "Why Is Same-Sex Sexual Behavior So Common in Animals?" *Observations* (blog). *Scientific American*. November 20, 2019. blogs.scientificamerican.com/observations/why-is-same-sex-sexual-behavior-so-common-in-animals.

Keeton, W. T. *Biological Sciences*. New York: W. W. Norton, 1978.

Kelch, August. "Bastardbegattung zwischen Melolontha vulgaris und Hippocastani." *Isis von Oken* 7 (1834).

Kimmerer, Robin Wall. *Braiding Sweetgrass: Indigenous Wisdom, Scientific Knowledge and the Teachings of Plants*. Minneapolis, MN: Milkweed Editions, 2013.

Kirkpatrick, R. C. "The Evolution of Human Homosexual Behavior." *Current Anthropology* 41, no. 3 (2000): 385–413.

Kota, M. V., E. M. Urquhart, and M. Zuk. "Spermatophore retention may accommodate sexual signal loss in Pacific field crickets." *Behavioral Ecology and Sociobiology* 74, 95 (2020).

Kristof, Nicholas. "Gay at Birth?" *New York Times*, October 25, 2003. www.nytimes.com/2003/10/25/opinion/gay-at-birth.html.

Lambert, Jonathan. "No 'Gay Gene': Study Looks at Genetic Basis of Sexuality." *Nature* 573, no. 7772 (2019): 14–15.

Lambert, M. R., T. Tran, A. Kilian, T. Ezaz, and D. K. Skelly. "Molecular Evidence for Sex Reversal in Wild Populations of Green Frogs (*Rana clamitans*)." *PeerJ* (2019).

Lambert, Max, and Melina Packer. "How Gendered Language Leads Scientists Astray." *Washington Post*, June 10, 2019. www.washingtonpost.com/outlook/2019/06/10/how-gendered-language-leads-scientists-astray/

Lehmiller, Justin. "Why Are We Searching for a 'Gay Gene'?" *Vice*, December 11, 2017. www.vice.com/en/article/zmym38/why-are-we-searching-for-a-gay-gene.

LeVay, Simon. *Gay, Straight, and the Reason Why: The Science of Sexual Orientation.* London, United Kingdom: Oxford University Press, 2017.

Levy, Michael. "Gay Rights Movement." In *Encyclopedia Britannica.* June 15, 2020. www .britannica.com/topic/gay-rights-movement.

Lewin, Roger. *Thread of Life: The Smithsonian Looks at Evolution.* Lanham, MD: Bernan, 1991.

Lorenz, Konrad, Michael Martys, and Angelika Tipler. *Here I Am—Where Are You?: The Behavior of the Greylag Goose.* New York: Harcourt Brace Jovanovich, 1991.

Lorenz, Konrad. "The Triumph Ceremony of the Greylag Goose, *Anser anser L.*" *Philosophical Transactions of the Royal Society B*, 251, no. 772 (1966): 477.

MacDonald, Helen. *Vesper Flights: New and Collected Essays.* London: Jonathan Cape, 2020.

MacFarlane, Geoff R., Simon P. Blomberg, Gisela Kaplan, and Lesley J. Rogers. "Same-Sex Sexual Behavior in Birds: Expression Is Related to Social Mating System and State of Development at Hatching." *Behavioral Ecology* 18, no. 1 (2006): 21–33.

Mann, Janet. "Establishing Trust: Socio-sexual Behaviour and the Development of Male-Male Bonds among Indian Ocean Bottlenose Dolphins." In *Homosexual Behaviour in Animals: An Evolutionary Perspective* (2006): 107–30.

Marwick, Alice, Mary L. Gray, and Mike Ananny. "Dolphins Are Just Gay Sharks." *Television & New Media* 15, no. 7 (2013): 627–47.

McHugh, S. "Queer (and) Animal Theories." *GLQ* 15, no. 1 (2009): 153–69.

McKie, Robin. "Chimps with Everything: Jane Goodall's 50 Years in the Jungle." *Guardian*, June 27, 2017. www.theguardian.com/science/2010/jun/27/jane-goodall-chimps -africa-interview.

Mills, Kim I. "Researchers Induce Homosexual Behavior in Male Fruit Flies." AP News. June 4, 1995. apnews.com/article/73111aafe4a205520a1548a14f4f840b.

Monk, J. D., E. Giglio, A. Kamath, M. R. Lambert, and C. E. McDonough. "An Alternative Hypothesis for the Evolution of Same-Sex Sexual Behaviour in Animals." *Nature Ecology & Evolution* 3, no. 12 (Dec. 2019): 1622–31.

Moyer, Jack T., and Akinobu Nakazono. "Protandrous Hermaphroditism in Six Species of the Anemonefish Genus Amphiprion in Japan." *Japanese Journal of Ichthyology* 25, no. 2 (1978): 101–6.

Muñoz, Roldan C., and Robert R. Warner. "A New Version of the Size-Advantage Hypothesis for Sex Change: Incorporating Sperm Competition and Size-Fecundity Skew." *American Naturalist* 161, no. 5 (2003): 749–61.

Murphy, Timothy F. "The search for the gay gene." *British Medical Journal* 330 (2005): 1033.

Nichols, Sam. "What's It Like Collecting Bull Cum for a Living?" *Vice*, June 29, 2017. www.vice.com/en/article/qv4y8b/whats-it-like-collecting-bull-cum-for-a-living.

O'Brien, Jodi. *Encyclopedia of Gender and Society*. Vol. 1. Los Angeles: Sage Publications, 2009.

Okasha, Samir. *The Stanford Encyclopedia of Philosophy* (Summer 2020 Edition). Edited by Edward N. Zalta. plato.stanford.edu/archives/sum2020/entries/altruism-biological.

"Overfishing." *National Geographic*. April 27, 2010. www.nationalgeographic.com/environment/article/critical-issues-overfishing.

Paredes, Raúl, and M. Baum. "Altered Sexual Partner Preference in Male Ferret Given Excitotoxic Lesions of the Preoptic Area/Anterior Hypothalamus." *Journal of Neuroscience* 15 (10) (1995): 6619–30.

Perkins, A., and J. Fitzgerald. "Is your ram a dud or a stud? Knowing the difference pays off." *Sheep!,* (July 1990): 4–5.

Perkins, A., and J. Fitzgerald. "Luteinizing Hormone, Testosterone, and Behavioral Response of Male-Oriented Rams to Estrous Ewes and Rams." *Journal of Animal Science* 70, no. 6 (1992): 1787–94.

Persons, Matthew H. "Field Observations of Simultaneous Double Mating in the Wolf Spider *Rabidosa punctulata* (Araneae: Lycosidae)." *Journal of Arachnology* 45, no. 2 (2017): 231–34.

Pickett, Brent. *The Stanford Encyclopedia of Philosophy* (Spring 2021 Edition). Edited by Edward N. Zalta. plato.stanford.edu/archives/spr2021/entries/homosexuality.

Pincemy, Gwénaëlle, F. Stephen Dobson, and Pierre Jouventin. "Homosexual Mating Displays in Penguins." *Ethology* 116, no. 12 (2010): 1210–16.

Plato. *Selected Dialogues of Plato: The Benjamin Jowett Translation.* London, United Kingdom: Random House Publishing Group, 2009.

Plutarch. *Select Lives by Plutarch.* Edinburgh: printed by A. Donaldson and J. Reid. For Alexander Donaldson, 1764. Eighteenth Century Collections Online (accessed August 18, 2021). link.gale.com/apps/doc/CW0101145318/ECCO?u=new64731&sid=bookmark-ECCO&xid=b4cb6923&pg=69.

Roberts, Brian. *The Breeding Behaviour of Penguins: With Special Reference to Pygoscelis papua* Forester. London: British Museum, 1940.

Robertson, D. R. "Social Control of Sex Reversal in a Coral-Reef Fish." *Science* 177, no. 4053 (1972): 1007–9.

"Roseate Tern." American Bird Conservancy. Accessed August 18, 2021. abcbirds.org /bird/roseate-tern.

Roughgarden, Joan. *Evolution's Rainbow: Diversity, Gender, and Sexuality in Nature and People.* Berkeley: University of California Press, 2013.

Rush, Elizabeth A. *Rising: Dispatches from the New American Shore.* Minneapolis, MN: Milkweed Editions, 2018.

Russell, Douglas G. D., William J. L. Sladen, and David G. Ainley. "Dr. George Murray Levick (1876–1956): Unpublished Notes on the Sexual Habits of the Adélie Penguin." *Polar Record* 48, no. 4 (2012): 387–93.

Sadovy de Mitcheson, Yvonne, and Liu Min. "Functional Hermaphroditism in Teleosts." *Fish & Fisheries* 9, no. 1 (2008): 1–43.

Salisbury, Joyce. *The Beast Within: Animals in the Middle Ages.* Hoboken, NJ: Taylor and Francis, 2012.

Sanders, Mark D., and Richard F. Maloney. "Causes of Mortality at Nests of Ground-Nesting Birds in the Upper Waitaki Basin, South Island, New Zealand: A 5-Year Video Study." *Biological Conservation* 106, no. 2 (2002): 225–36.

Saravi, Fernando. "The Elusive Search for a 'Gay Gene': A Gay Brain?," in *Tall Tales about the Mind and Brain.* London: Oxford University Press (2007): 461–77.

Scharf, Inon, and Oliver Y. Martin. "Same-Sex Sexual Behavior in Insects and Arachnids: Prevalence, Causes, and Consequences." *Behavioral Ecology and Sociobiology* 67, no. 11 (2013): 1719–30.

Schatten, Gerald, and Heide Schatten. "The Energetic Egg." *Sciences* 23, no. 5 (1983): 28–35.

Scully, Matthew. *Dominion: The Power of Man, the Suffering of Animals, and the Call to Mercy.* New York: St. Martin's Press, 2003.

Shine, Richard, Tracy Langkilde, and Robert T. Mason. "Confusion within 'Mating Balls' of Garter Snakes: Does Misdirected Courtship Impose Selection on Male Tactics?" *Animal Behaviour* 66, no. 6 (2003): 1011–17.

Slagsvold, Tore, and Glenn-Peter Sætre. "Evolution of Plumage Color in Male Pied Flycatchers (*Ficedula hypoleuca*): Evidence for Female Mimicry." *Evolution* 45, no. 4 (1991): 910–17.

Smith, Kat. "Life as a Bull Stud: What Really Happens in Cattle Breeding?" Livekindly. Accessed March 29, 2021. www.livekindly.co/bull-stud-what-really-happens-cattle-breeding.

Smolker, Rachel A., Andrew F. Richards, Richard C. Connor, and John W. Pepper. "Sex Differences in Patterns of Association among Indian Ocean Bottlenose Dolphins." *Behaviour* 123, nos. 1–2 (1992): 38–69.

Sommer, Volker, and Paul L. Vasey. *Homosexual Behaviour in Animals: An Evolutionary Perspective*. Cambridge: Cambridge University Press, 2006.

Terry, Jennifer. "'Unnatural Acts' in Nature: The Scientific Fascination with Queer Animals." *GLQ* 6, no. 2 (2000): 151–93.

Thomas, Jack Ward, R. M. Robinson, and R. G. Marburger. "Social Behavior in a White-Tailed Deer Herd Containing Hypogonadal Males." *Journal of Mammalogy* 46, no. 2 (1965): 314–27.

University of Illinois at Chicago. "In Fruit Flies, Homosexuality Is Biological but Not Hard-Wired, Study Shows." Science Daily. December 10, 2007. www.sciencedaily.com/releases/2007/12/071210094541.htm.

Vasey, P. L. "Same-Sex Sexual Partner Preference in Hormonally and Neurologically Unmanipulated Animals." *Annual Review of Sex Research* 13 (2002): 141–79.

Velocci, Beans. "The Battle over Trans Rights Is about Power, Not Science." *Washington Post*, October 29, 2018. www.washingtonpost.com/outlook/2018/10/29/battle-over-trans-rights-is-about-power-not-science.

Vines, Gail. "Queer Creatures." *New Scientist*. August 6, 1999. www.newscientist.com/article/mg16321985-000-queer-creatures.

Wareham, Jamie. "Murdered, Suffocated and Burned Alive—350 Transgender People Killed in 2020." *Forbes*, November 11, 2020. www.forbes.com/sites/jamiewareham /2020/11/11/350-transgender-people-have-been-murdered-in-2020-transgender-day -of-remembrance-list/?sh=33dee7f565a6.

Warner, Robert R. "Mating Behavior and Hermaphroditism in Coral Reef Fishes: The Diverse Forms of Sexuality Found among Tropical Marine Fishes Can Be Viewed as Adaptations to Their Equally Diverse Mating Systems." *American Scientist* 72, no. 2 (1984): 128–36.

Warner, Robert R., and D. Ross Robertson. "Sexual patterns in the labroid fishes of the western Caribbean, I: the wrasses (Labridae)." *Smithsonian Contributions to Zoology* (1978): 1–27.

Webb, Christine E., Peter Woodford, and Elise Huchard. "The Study That Made Rats Jump for Joy, and Then Killed Them." *BioEssays* 42, no. 6 (2020).

Weiß, Brigitte M. "Alternative Social and Reproductive Strategies." In *The Social Life of Greylag Geese: Patterns, Mechanisms and Evolutionary Function in an Avian Model System*, edited by Brigitte M. Weiß, Isabella B. R. Scheiber, Josef Hemetsberger, and Kurt Kotrschal. Cambridge: Cambridge University Press, 2013: 88–104.

Weyand, Logan K., E. Frances Cassirer, Gretchen E. Kaufman, and Thomas E. Besser. "*Mycoplasma ovipneumoniae* Strains associated with Pneumonia Outbreaks in North American Bighorn Sheep." In *Biennial Symposium of the Northern Wild Sheep and Goat Council* 20 (2016): 89–97.

Wilcox, Christie. "The Mechanics of Dolphin Sex: All the Dirty Details You Need to Know." *Discover*, October 10, 2017. www.discovermagazine.com/planet-earth/the-mechanics -of-dolphin-sex-all-the-dirty-details-you-need-to-know.

Wong, Wilson. "Gay Male Penguins Steal Lesbian Couple's Eggs at Dutch Zoo." NBC News, October 3, 2020. www.nbcnews.com/feature/nbc-out/gay-male-penguins-steal -lesbian-couple-s-eggs-dutch-zoo-n1244575.

Woods, Vanessa. *Bonobo Handshake: A Memoir of Love and Adventure in the Congo.* New York: Gotham Books, 2010.

Young, Lindsay C., and Eric A. VanderWerf. "Adaptive Value of Same-Sex Pairing in Laysan Albatross." *Proceedings of the Royal Society B: Biological Sciences* 281, no. 1775 (2014): 20132473.

Zuk, M. "Family values in black and white." *Nature* 439, 917 (2006).

INDEX

ELIOT SCHREFER is a *New York Times* bestselling author and has twice been a finalist for the National Book Award in Young People's Literature. His nonfiction has appeared in the *New York Times* and *Discover* magazine, and his novels include *The Darkness Outside Us*, *Endangered*, and the Lost Rainforest series. He is on the faculty of the Hamline University and Fairleigh Dickinson University MFA programs in creative writing, is getting an MA in animal studies at NYU, and reviews books for *USA Today*. Visit him online at www.eliotschrefer.com.

PRONOUNS: **HE/HIM**
TWITTER: **@ELIOTSCHREFER**

JULES ZUCKERBERG is a queer trans illustrator. They grew up in the woods of NY, where they first discovered their love for observing and drawing animals, developing a huge soft spot for insects, amphibians, and anyone else that might be hiding under a log. As they grew into an adult and embraced their own queerness, their art developed alongside, evolving to embody themes of identity through both autobiographical and educational content. *Queer Ducks* represents a deeply exciting collision between two topics near and dear to Jules's wild gay heart.

PRONOUNS: **THEY/THEM**
TWITTER **@JULESZUCKERBERG**